Unraveling the Antagonisms of Regional Players

Table of Contents

Unraveling the Antagonisms of Regional Players

By Roberto Miguel Rodriguez

Brief Description of the Book

The Antagonisms or Jealousies of Regional Middle Powers

In this chapter, we will explore the underlying antagonisms and jealousies that exist among regional middle powers. We will delve into the historical context and analyze the factors that contribute to these rivalries. By examining case studies and diplomatic records, we will uncover the root causes of these conflicts and shed light on their impact on regional stability.

The Impact of Regional Middle Powers on Global Diplomacy and Power Dynamics

This chapter aims to analyze the influence of regional middle powers on global diplomacy and power dynamics. We will examine how these middle powers navigate the complex international arena, influencing alliances and shaping global policies. By studying their diplomatic strategies and initiatives, we will gain insights into the significant role they play in shaping the international order.

Competition for Regional Influence Among Middle Powers

This chapter focuses on the competition for regional influence among middle powers. We will explore the tactics employed by these powers to assert their dominance in their respective regions. By examining case studies and analyzing geopolitical dynamics, we will uncover the strategies and power struggles that unfold in the pursuit of regional influence.

Economic Rivalries and Trade Disputes Among Regional Middle Powers

In this chapter, we will delve into the economic rivalries and trade disputes that arise among regional middle powers. We will examine the impact of these conflicts on regional cooperation and explore potential avenues for resolution. By analyzing economic data and trade policies, we will provide a comprehensive understanding of the complexities of economic rivalries among middle powers.

Territorial Disputes and Conflicts Between Regional Middle Powers

This chapter will focus on the territorial disputes and conflicts that arise between regional middle powers. We will examine the historical context and political dynamics that contribute to these tensions. By studying the legal frameworks and diplomatic negotiations, we will assess the implications of these conflicts on regional stability.

Political Rivalries and Power Struggles Among Regional Middle Powers

This chapter will analyze the political rivalries and power struggles that characterize the relationships between regional middle powers. We will explore the ideological differences and competing visions that fuel these conflicts. By examining case studies and political campaigns, we will provide insights into the underlying dynamics of political rivalries among middle powers.

Security Alliances and Counterbalancing Strategies of Regional Middle Powers

In this chapter, we will examine the security alliances and counterbalancing strategies adopted by regional middle powers. We will analyze how these powers form alliances and coalitions to safeguard their interests and enhance their security. By studying military agreements and defense policies, we will assess the effectiveness of these strategies in maintaining regional stability.

Cultural and Identity Clashes Among Regional Middle Powers

This chapter explores the cultural and identity clashes that arise among regional middle powers. We will examine the role of cultural differences, historical grievances, and national identities in fueling these conflicts. By analyzing social and cultural data, we will provide insights into the complexities of cultural clashes among middle powers.

Role of Regional Middle Powers in Regional Integration and Cooperation

This chapter will focus on the role of regional middle powers in regional integration and cooperation. We will analyze their contributions to regional organizations and initiatives aimed at fostering cooperation. By studying case studies and diplomatic records, we will assess the impact of middle powers on regional integration and cooperation.

Energy Resources and Competition Among Regional Middle Powers

In this chapter, we will explore the competition among regional middle powers for energy resources. We will analyze the impact of these competitions on regional stability and global energy dynamics. By examining energy policies and resource distribution, we will provide insights into the complexities of energy rivalries among middle powers.

Implications of Regional Middle Power Conflicts on Global Security and Stability

This final chapter will assess the implications of conflicts among regional middle powers on global security and stability. We will analyze the ripple effects of these conflicts on the international order and potential pathways for resolution. By studying historical precedents and geopolitical dynamics, we will provide a comprehensive understanding of the global impact of regional middle power conflicts.

Chapter 1: Introduction

Overview of the book

"Middle Power Maneuvers: Unraveling the Antagonisms and Jealousies of Regional Players" is an in-depth exploration of the complex dynamics and interactions among regional middle powers in the global arena. This book provides a comprehensive analysis of the various factors that contribute to the antagonisms and jealousies among these players, and examines their impact on global diplomacy, power dynamics, and regional stability.

Addressed to diplomats, economists, and strategists, this book offers a unique perspective on the intricate relationships between regional middle powers. It delves into the competition for regional influence, economic rivalries and trade disputes, territorial conflicts, political rivalries and power struggles, security alliances, cultural clashes, and the role of these powers in regional integration and cooperation.

The book sheds light on the economic and political motivations that drive these middle powers to vie for regional influence. It explores the implications of their conflicts on global security and stability, emphasizing the need for effective diplomacy and strategic maneuvering to mitigate potential threats.

Readers will gain a deeper understanding of the energy resources and competition among regional middle powers, which often fuel tensions and rivalries. The book analyzes the intricate web of alliances and counterbalancing strategies employed by these powers to secure their interests and maintain regional stability.

In addition, the book explores the cultural and identity clashes that further complicate relations among regional middle powers. By examining the underlying causes of these conflicts, it offers insights into potential pathways for conflict resolution and cooperation.

Ultimately, "Middle Power Maneuvers" provides a comprehensive overview of the diverse challenges and opportunities presented by regional middle powers. By unraveling the complex antagonisms and jealousies that underpin their interactions, this book equips diplomats, economists, and strategists with the knowledge and tools necessary to navigate the intricate landscape of global diplomacy and power dynamics.

Importance of studying regional middle powers

In the complex world of global politics, the significance of regional middle powers cannot be understated. These countries, often overlooked in favor of major superpowers, play a crucial role in shaping international relations and power dynamics. Understanding the importance of studying regional middle powers is essential for diplomats, economists, and strategists alike.

One key aspect that warrants attention is the antagonisms and jealousies that arise among regional middle powers. These nations often find themselves entangled in rivalries, driven by competing interests and aspirations. By comprehending the underlying causes and dynamics of these conflicts, diplomats can work towards effective conflict resolution, cooperation, and diplomacy.

Furthermore, the impact of regional middle powers on global diplomacy and power dynamics is significant. These countries possess the capability to influence and shape international policies, particularly within their respective regions. By studying their strategies, economists and strategists can identify trends and develop insights into how global power structures are formed and reshaped.

Competition for regional influence among middle powers is another crucial area that demands attention. As these nations vie for dominance, economic rivalries and trade disputes often arise. By understanding the root causes of these conflicts, economists can analyze their impact on global trade and economic stability, providing valuable insights for policymakers and businesses.

Territorial disputes and conflicts between regional middle powers present further challenges. These conflicts have the potential to escalate and destabilize entire regions. Diplomats and strategists must study these conflicts to develop effective mediation strategies and ensure regional stability.

Political rivalries and power struggles are also common among regional middle powers. By examining the motivations and actions of these nations, diplomats and strategists can better navigate the intricate web of alliances and counterbalancing strategies.

Cultural and identity clashes among regional middle powers should not be overlooked. These conflicts often fuel animosities and hinder regional integration and cooperation. By studying the underlying cultural dynamics, diplomats can facilitate dialogue and understanding, promoting harmony and cooperation.

The role of regional middle powers in regional integration and cooperation is of utmost importance. Understanding their interests, capabilities, and limitations is essential for designing effective integration strategies and fostering cooperation.

Energy resources and competition among regional middle powers are critical aspects that economists and strategists must analyze. The control and distribution of energy resources have significant geopolitical implications. By studying the strategies employed by regional middle powers, economists can predict trends and anticipate the impact on global energy security.

Finally, the implications of conflicts among regional middle powers on global security and stability must be thoroughly examined. These conflicts have far-reaching consequences, and understanding their potential impact is crucial for diplomats, economists, and strategists.

In conclusion, studying regional middle powers is of paramount importance for diplomats, economists, and strategists. By comprehending the antagonisms, impacts, and implications of these nations, professionals can navigate the complex landscape of global politics, foster cooperation, and ensure stability.

Scope and objectives of the book

Scope and Objectives of the Book: "Middle Power Maneuvers: Unraveling the Antagonisms and Jealousies of Regional Players"

Introduction:

In today's complex global landscape, regional middle powers have emerged as key actors in international relations. This book, "Middle Power Maneuvers: Unraveling the Antagonisms and Jealousies of Regional Players," aims to provide a comprehensive analysis of the various dynamics, conflicts, and rivalries among these middle powers. Targeted at diplomats, economists, and strategists, this subchapter outlines the scope and objectives of the book, offering a glimpse into the crucial themes that will be explored.

Understanding the Antagonisms and Jealousies:

The book delves deep into the antagonisms and jealousies that exist among regional middle powers. It examines the historical, political, and cultural factors that contribute to these rivalries and their implications for global diplomacy and power dynamics. By unraveling the intricacies of these conflicts, the book seeks to provide valuable insights for policymakers and analysts.

Exploring Competition for Regional Influence:

One of the key objectives of this book is to shed light on the intense competition for regional influence among middle powers. It investigates the strategies employed, alliances formed, and counterbalancing measures taken by these players to enhance their regional standing. The book also explores how this competition impacts regional integration, cooperation, and stability.

Analyzing Economic Rivalries and Trade Disputes:

Economic rivalries and trade disputes often shape the relationships between regional middle powers. This book aims to examine the underlying causes of such conflicts and their consequences for the global economy. It explores the role of energy resources in these rivalries and the implications they have for regional and global stability.

Unpacking Territorial Disputes and Conflicts:

Territorial disputes and conflicts are significant sources of tension among regional middle powers. This subchapter delves into the historical and geopolitical aspects of these conflicts, analyzing their impact on regional security and stability. It also examines the role of cultural and identity clashes in exacerbating these disputes.

Understanding Political Rivalries and Power Struggles:

Political rivalries and power struggles often define the relationships between regional middle powers. This book aims to provide an in-depth analysis of the political dynamics that drive these conflicts and their implications for regional and global governance. It explores how these rivalries influence decision-making processes and shape alliances.

Conclusion:

"Middle Power Maneuvers: Unraveling the Antagonisms and Jealousies of Regional Players" offers a comprehensive exploration of the multifaceted dynamics among regional middle powers. By addressing various themes such as economic rivalries, territorial disputes, political power struggles, and cultural clashes, the book aims to provide a nuanced understanding of these conflicts and their implications for global security and stability. Diplomats, economists, and strategists will find this book an invaluable resource for navigating the complex world of regional middle powers.

Chapter 2: The Antagonisms or Jealousies of Regional Middle Powers

Definition and characteristics of regional middle powers

In this subchapter, we will delve into the definition and characteristics of regional middle powers, shedding light on their roles and significance in global diplomacy and power dynamics. This knowledge is essential for diplomats, economists, and strategists seeking a comprehensive understanding of the complex dynamics between regional players.

Regional middle powers can be defined as states that possess a significant level of influence and capabilities within their respective regions, but fall short of being major global powers. These middle powers often have the potential to shape regional outcomes, but lack the comprehensive reach and capabilities to exert influence on a global scale.

Characteristics that distinguish regional middle powers include their geographical positioning, economic strength, political stability, and diplomatic influence. These states often serve as regional economic hubs, attracting investment and fostering trade relationships within their areas of influence. They possess a diverse range of industries and resources, which further enhances their economic prowess.

Regional middle powers also exhibit a level of political stability and institutional strength that enables them to play an influential role in regional affairs. They are often seen as mediators or facilitators in regional conflicts and disputes, providing a platform for dialogue and negotiation.

Furthermore, these middle powers engage in strategic alliances and counterbalancing strategies to safeguard their interests and maintain regional stability. Through these alliances, they aim to balance power dynamics and prevent any single regional player from dominating the region.

However, competition among regional middle powers is also prevalent, particularly in terms of economic rivalries, trade disputes, territorial conflicts, and political power struggles. These dynamics can create tensions and antagonisms, leading to conflict and instability within the region.

Cultural and identity clashes are another aspect that characterizes the relationships among regional middle powers. Differences in historical narratives, religious beliefs, and cultural practices can often fuel animosity and hinder regional integration and cooperation.

The implications of conflicts and rivalries among regional middle powers extend beyond the region itself. They have a significant impact on global security and stability, as they can potentially escalate into broader conflicts or draw major global powers into regional disputes.

In conclusion, regional middle powers play a crucial role in shaping global diplomacy and power dynamics. Understanding their definition and characteristics is essential for diplomats, economists, and strategists, as it provides insights into the complex interactions and rivalries among regional players. By comprehending these dynamics, we can better navigate the challenges and opportunities presented by regional middle powers in today's interconnected world.

Historical context of antagonisms and jealousies among regional middle powers

The historical context of antagonisms and jealousies among regional middle powers is a complex and intriguing subject that holds significant relevance for diplomats, economists, and strategists. This subchapter aims to unravel the underlying factors that have shaped the relationships between these regional players and the implications it has had on global diplomacy and power dynamics.

Competition for regional influence among middle powers has been a recurring theme throughout history. From ancient civilizations vying for dominance to modern-day nation-states, the struggle for regional supremacy has often led to tensions and rivalries. Historical examples include the power struggles between Greece and Persia in ancient times, the European colonial rivalries in the 19th century, and the Cold War proxy conflicts fought between the United States and the Soviet Union.

Economic rivalries and trade disputes among regional middle powers have also played a significant role in shaping antagonisms. Economic competition, access to resources, and trade imbalances have frequently sparked conflicts and strained relations between neighboring countries. For instance, the economic rivalry between India and China in South Asia has led to disputes over trade routes, market access, and investments, impacting regional stability.

Territorial disputes and conflicts between regional middle powers have often been a source of contention and animosity. Historical conflicts such as the Arab-Israeli conflict, the India-Pakistan territorial disputes, and the ongoing disputes in the South China Sea highlight the deep-rooted antagonisms arising from competing claims over land, maritime boundaries, and strategic resources.

Political rivalries and power struggles among regional middle powers have shaped the dynamics of their relationships. Quests for regional hegemony, ideological differences, and power vacuums have fueled political rivalries that often manifest in proxy wars, diplomatic maneuvering, and strategic alliances. Examples include the power struggle between Saudi Arabia and Iran in the Middle East and the historical rivalry between Brazil and Argentina in South America.

Security alliances and counterbalancing strategies among regional middle powers have been employed to safeguard their interests and maintain a balance of power. Historical examples include the formation of alliances like NATO and the Warsaw Pact during the Cold War, as well as the current ASEAN Regional Forum in Southeast Asia. These alliances seek to counterbalance the influence of dominant powers and prevent regional power imbalances.

Cultural and identity clashes among regional middle powers have also contributed to antagonisms and jealousies. Differences in religious, ethnic, and cultural identities have often fueled conflicts and created divisions among neighboring nations. The historical animosities between India and Pakistan, rooted in religious and cultural differences, exemplify this aspect.

The role of regional middle powers in regional integration and cooperation is another critical aspect to consider. While antagonisms and jealousies have often hindered collaboration, regional middle powers have also played significant roles in fostering integration and cooperation. The European Union is a prime example of regional integration driven by middle powers seeking to overcome historical rivalries and promote common interests.

Energy resources and competition among regional middle powers have become increasingly significant in the modern era. The quest for control over energy resources, such as oil and gas reserves, has intensified rivalries and strained relations between regional players. The competition for energy resources in the Middle East and the South China Sea has been a major driver of tensions and conflicts.

The implications of regional middle power conflicts on global security and stability cannot be underestimated. These conflicts have the potential to escalate into larger regional or even global confrontations, affecting diplomatic relations, trade, and economic stability. The historical precedent of conflicts between regional middle powers escalating into wider conflicts, such as World War I, underscores the importance of understanding and managing these antagonisms.

In conclusion, the historical context of antagonisms and jealousies among regional middle powers is a multifaceted subject that has shaped global diplomacy and power dynamics. Understanding these historical factors is crucial for diplomats, economists, and strategists as they navigate the complexities of regional relationships and work towards global peace and stability.

Case studies: Examples of antagonisms and jealousies among regional middle powers

Introduction:

In this subchapter, we will examine several case studies that highlight the various antagonisms and jealousies among regional middle powers. By delving into these specific examples, we aim to provide diplomats, economists, and strategists with valuable insights into the dynamics of power struggles, rivalries, and conflicts that shape the global landscape. These case studies will shed light on the impact of regional middle powers on global diplomacy, the competition for regional influence, economic rivalries, territorial disputes, political struggles, security alliances, cultural clashes, and the role of middle powers in regional integration and cooperation. Furthermore, we will also explore the implications of these conflicts on global security and stability.

Case Study 1: The South China Sea Dispute

The South China Sea dispute involving China, Vietnam, the Philippines, and other regional middle powers underscores the intense competition for regional influence. This territorial conflict has led to heightened tensions, military build-ups, and economic rivalries, as these middle powers vie for control over strategic resources and trade routes.

Case Study 2: India-Pakistan Rivalry

The long-standing antagonism between India and Pakistan serves as a prime example of political rivalries and power struggles among regional middle powers. Their territorial disputes, particularly over Kashmir, have resulted in numerous conflicts, nuclear proliferation, and ongoing security concerns.

Case Study 3: Brazil-Argentina Economic Rivalry

The economic rivalry between Brazil and Argentina highlights the complexities of trade disputes among regional middle powers. These two nations frequently engage in protectionist measures, tariff wars, and currency devaluations, as they vie for dominance in the South American market.

Case Study 4: Saudi Arabia-Iran Cultural Clashes

The cultural and identity clashes between Saudi Arabia and Iran manifest in their proxy wars and sectarian struggles across the Middle East. This profound regional antagonism has exacerbated religious tensions, fueling conflicts in countries like Syria, Yemen, and Lebanon.

Conclusion:

These case studies serve as vivid illustrations of the antagonisms and jealousies among regional middle powers. By analyzing these conflicts, diplomats, economists, and strategists can gain a comprehensive understanding of the complex dynamics that shape global diplomacy and power struggles. The impact of these rivalries on regional integration, energy resources, and global security underscores the need for effective diplomatic engagement and conflict resolution mechanisms. As middle powers continue to shape the international order, it is crucial for policymakers to navigate these complexities in order to foster stability, cooperation, and sustainable development on a global scale.

Sub-chapter heading

Sub-chapter heading: The Impact of Regional Middle Powers on Global Diplomacy and Power Dynamics

In this sub-chapter, we will delve into the profound implications that the antagonisms and jealousies of regional middle powers have on global diplomacy and power dynamics. As diplomats, economists, and strategists, understanding these dynamics is crucial in navigating the complex web of international relations.

Regional middle powers, often overlooked in the global arena, possess the potential to significantly influence the balance of power on a global scale. Their actions, whether cooperative or competitive, shape the trajectory of international relations and have far-reaching consequences.

Competition for regional influence among middle powers is a key aspect that must be analyzed. As these countries vie for dominance within their respective regions, they engage in economic rivalries and trade disputes. These conflicts not only impact the economic stability of the regions but also have global repercussions, affecting trade flows, investment patterns, and even global economic growth.

Territorial disputes and conflicts between regional middle powers also contribute to the volatility of global diplomacy. These conflicts, rooted in historical, cultural, and political rivalries, pose significant challenges to the maintenance of peace and stability. The strategies employed by middle powers to assert their territorial claims can lead to security alliances and counterbalancing efforts, further complicating the power dynamics in the region.

Cultural and identity clashes among regional middle powers are another dimension that cannot be ignored. These clashes, often fueled by historical grievances and nationalistic sentiments, have the potential to escalate tensions and hinder regional integration and cooperation efforts. Understanding the underlying cultural complexities is crucial in formulating effective diplomatic strategies.

Furthermore, the role of regional middle powers in regional integration and cooperation cannot be undermined. These countries hold significant influence in shaping regional organizations and initiatives, either through their active participation or deliberate obstruction. Their actions can either foster collaboration or exacerbate existing rivalries, impacting the overall stability and progress of the region.

Lastly, energy resources and competition among regional middle powers warrant careful analysis. As countries scramble for control over valuable energy resources, conflicts and tensions arise. These struggles not only impact regional stability but also have global implications, as energy security is a vital concern for all nations.

In conclusion, the antagonisms and jealousies among regional middle powers have a profound impact on global diplomacy and power dynamics. As diplomats, economists, and strategists, it is essential to understand these dynamics and their implications on various aspects such as trade, security, cultural integration, and global stability. Only through a comprehensive understanding can we navigate the complexities of international relations and seek avenues for cooperation and peace.

Sub-chapter heading

Sub-chapter Heading: Understanding the Antagonisms and Jealousies of Regional Middle Powers

As diplomats, economists, and strategists, it is crucial to comprehend the complex dynamics of regional middle powers and their impact on global diplomacy. This sub-chapter aims to unravel the antagonisms and jealousies that often shape the behavior of these influential players on the world stage.

Regional middle powers, characterized by their significant economic, political, and military capabilities, frequently find themselves locked in competition for regional influence. This chapter delves into the various factors that drive this competition, such as historical rivalries, ideological differences, and aspirations for regional leadership.

Economic rivalries and trade disputes are common among regional middle powers. This sub-chapter explores the intricate web of economic interdependence and the consequences of trade conflicts, as well as the strategies employed by these powers to gain a competitive edge in the global market.

Territorial disputes and conflicts between regional middle powers have the potential to escalate into full-scale conflicts. By examining historical and contemporary cases, this sub-chapter sheds light on the roots of these disputes and their implications for regional stability and global security.

Political rivalries and power struggles within the region are also prevalent among middle powers. The chapter uncovers the underlying motivations behind these struggles, including the desire for regional dominance, access to resources, and the pursuit of national interests.

Security alliances and counterbalancing strategies employed by regional middle powers are significant determinants of power dynamics. This sub-chapter investigates the intricate web of alliances and examines how they shape regional security architecture and influence global politics.

Cultural and identity clashes are often at the heart of regional middle power conflicts. The chapter explores how divergent cultural norms, historical grievances, and religious differences contribute to these clashes, and the potential implications for regional integration and cooperation.

The role of regional middle powers in regional integration and cooperation cannot be underestimated. This sub-chapter analyzes the efforts made by these powers to foster closer ties, promote economic cooperation, and enhance regional security.

Furthermore, the competition for energy resources among regional middle powers is a critical aspect of their maneuvering. This chapter explores the implications of this competition on energy security, regional stability, and global energy markets.

Ultimately, this sub-chapter delves into the implications of regional middle power conflicts on global security and stability. By understanding the underlying dynamics of these conflicts, diplomats, economists, and strategists can better navigate the complexities of global diplomacy and contribute to the pursuit of peace and stability in the international arena.

Chapter 3: The Impact of Regional Middle Powers on Global Diplomacy and Power Dynamics

Rise of regional middle powers and their influence on global politics

In recent years, the international arena has witnessed a significant shift in power dynamics, with the rise of regional middle powers exerting a newfound influence on global politics. This subchapter explores the various dimensions of this phenomenon, shedding light on the antagonisms, impacts, and rivalries that have emerged among these regional players. Aimed at diplomats, economists, and strategists, this chapter provides a comprehensive analysis of the complex dynamics at play.

The antagonisms or jealousies of regional middle powers are a central theme explored in this subchapter. As these powers gain prominence, they increasingly vie for influence and control within their respective regions. This competition often gives rise to territorial disputes, economic rivalries, and political power struggles. By delving into these issues, this chapter seeks to offer valuable insights into the underlying dynamics that drive these conflicts.

Furthermore, this subchapter examines the impact of regional middle powers on global diplomacy and power dynamics. As these powers assert their influence, they challenge the traditional dominance of global powers, reshaping the balance of power. The chapter explores the strategies employed by these middle powers to counterbalance larger players and forge security alliances, thereby altering the dynamics of diplomatic relations at a global level.

Economic rivalries and trade disputes among regional middle powers also play a crucial role in shaping global politics. This subchapter delves into the ways in which these economic rivalries impact global trade and the broader geopolitical landscape. By exploring the implications of these disputes, it provides a nuanced understanding of the intricate relationship between economic competition and global power dynamics.

Territorial disputes and conflicts between regional middle powers are another key aspect explored in this subchapter. By analyzing the specific challenges posed by these conflicts, the chapter sheds light on their implications for global security and stability. It also considers how these disputes intersect with cultural and identity clashes, further complicating the dynamics of regional rivalries.

Moreover, this subchapter investigates the role of regional middle powers in regional integration and cooperation. These powers often play a vital role in fostering regional cooperation and integration initiatives, acting as pivotal mediators and facilitators. By examining their contributions, the chapter offers insights into the potential for regional middle powers to shape the future of global governance.

Additionally, the subchapter explores the competition among regional middle powers for energy resources. As these powers seek to secure their energy needs, they engage in strategic partnerships and rivalries that have far-reaching implications for global energy security. By analyzing this dimension, the chapter provides a comprehensive understanding of the complex interplay between energy resources and global power dynamics.

In conclusion, this subchapter sheds light on the rise of regional middle powers and their profound influence on global politics. By exploring the antagonisms, impacts, and rivalries among these powers, it offers valuable insights for diplomats, economists, and strategists. From economic rivalries to territorial disputes, this chapter unravels the intricate dynamics that shape the role of regional middle powers in the evolving global landscape.

Regional middle powers' role in shaping international institutions and norms

Regional middle powers play a crucial role in shaping international institutions and norms. These countries, despite not being global superpowers, possess significant economic, political, and military capabilities that enable them to influence global diplomacy and power dynamics.

One of the key aspects of regional middle powers is their competition for regional influence. These countries often engage in diplomatic maneuvering, economic partnerships, and alliances to expand their sphere of influence within their respective regions. Their actions have a direct impact on the balance of power and regional stability, as they seek to assert their interests and shape the regional order.

Economic rivalries and trade disputes are also common among regional middle powers. These countries compete for access to markets, resources, and investments, leading to tensions and conflicts. Their economic interdependence makes these disputes particularly challenging to resolve, as they can have far-reaching implications for regional and global economic stability.

Territorial disputes and conflicts also arise between regional middle powers, often fueled by historical grievances and nationalistic sentiments. These conflicts pose significant challenges to regional stability and often require diplomatic efforts to find peaceful resolutions.

Political rivalries and power struggles among regional middle powers further complicate the dynamics within and between regions. These countries vie for regional leadership and influence, engaging in diplomatic alliances and rivalries to advance their political agendas. Such power struggles can lead to tensions and conflicts that have broader implications for global security.

Security alliances and counterbalancing strategies are common among regional middle powers as they seek to protect their interests and counter perceived threats from other regional players. These alliances can shape the security architecture of a region and impact the balance of power.

Cultural and identity clashes also exist among regional middle powers, as diverse ethnic and cultural groups vie for recognition and influence. These clashes can create tensions and conflicts within and between countries, affecting regional stability and cooperation.

Regional middle powers also play a crucial role in regional integration and cooperation efforts. They often serve as mediators and facilitators in regional conflicts, promoting dialogue and cooperation to resolve disputes and promote peace and stability.

The competition for energy resources is another area of contention among regional middle powers. As energy demands increase, these countries vie for control over energy resources, leading to competition and potential conflicts that can have global implications.

The conflicts and rivalries among regional middle powers have significant implications for global security and stability. These tensions can escalate into larger conflicts, involving other global powers and disrupting regional and global order.

In conclusion, regional middle powers play a critical role in shaping international institutions and norms. Their actions and competition for influence have far-reaching implications for global diplomacy, power dynamics, and regional stability. It is essential for diplomats, economists, and strategists to understand and navigate the complexities of these regional dynamics to promote peace, stability, and cooperation in a rapidly changing global landscape.

Sub-chapter heading

Sub-chapter Heading: The Impact of Regional Middle Powers on Global Diplomacy and Power Dynamics

In this sub-chapter, we delve into the intricate web of regional middle powers and their significant influence on the global diplomatic landscape and power dynamics. As diplomats, economists, and strategists, it is crucial to comprehend the antagonisms and jealousies that arise among these regional players and the implications they hold for global security and stability.

The world today is witnessing a paradigm shift in power dynamics, where regional middle powers increasingly assert their influence on the global stage. These actors, while not possessing the sheer might of superpowers, possess unique characteristics that enable them to shape global diplomacy in profound ways.

One of the primary areas of concern is the competition for regional influence among middle powers. As regional players vie for dominance, their rivalries can have far-reaching consequences, both regionally and globally. Economic rivalries and trade disputes among regional middle powers have the potential to disrupt global trade flows and hinder economic cooperation. Similarly, territorial disputes and conflicts between these actors can escalate tensions, leading to instability in the regions they inhabit.

Moreover, political rivalries and power struggles among regional middle powers can result in diplomatic gridlocks and impede progress on critical global issues. To counterbalance these challenges, security alliances and counterbalancing strategies are often employed by middle powers, shaping the geopolitics of various regions.

However, it is not merely strategic and economic interests that drive these conflicts. Cultural and identity clashes among regional middle powers also play a significant role, as differing values and ideologies create fault lines that can be exploited by external actors. Additionally, the role of regional middle powers in regional integration and cooperation cannot be understated. Their participation in multilateral organizations and initiatives contributes to collective efforts in addressing shared challenges and fostering regional stability.

Furthermore, the competition for energy resources among regional middle powers adds another layer of complexity to their interactions. As the demand for energy resources increases, these actors engage in fierce competition, affecting global energy markets and exacerbating geopolitical tensions.

In conclusion, the antagonisms and jealousies of regional middle powers have a profound impact on global diplomacy and power dynamics. Understanding these dynamics is essential for diplomats, economists, and strategists to navigate the complex landscape of international relations. By comprehending the implications of these conflicts, we can work towards promoting global security, stability, and cooperation.

Sub-chapter heading

Sub-chapter Heading: Understanding the Antagonisms and Jealousies of Regional Middle Powers

Introduction:

In the complex landscape of global diplomacy and power dynamics, regional middle powers play a crucial role in shaping the international order. This sub-chapter delves into the various antagonisms and jealousies that arise among these regional players and explores their impact on global diplomacy, power dynamics, and security. By examining the competition for regional influence, economic rivalries, territorial disputes, political rivalries, security alliances, cultural clashes, and their role in regional integration, this chapter seeks to unravel the intricate web of middle power maneuvers.

Competition for Regional Influence:

Regional middle powers often find themselves locked in intense competition for regional influence. As they seek to assert their dominance and expand their spheres of influence, rivalries emerge, fostering a dynamic environment of power struggles and political maneuvering. This sub-chapter analyzes the drivers of this competition, the strategies employed, and the implications for regional stability and global diplomacy.

Economic Rivalries and Trade Disputes:

The interplay of economic rivalries and trade disputes among regional middle powers presents a unique set of challenges. As these powers vie for economic supremacy, tensions can escalate, leading to trade barriers, protectionist policies, and economic conflicts. By examining case studies and analyzing the economic dimensions of middle power rivalries, this sub-chapter sheds light on the economic dynamics that shape regional power struggles.

Territorial Disputes and Conflicts:

Territorial disputes are a common source of friction among regional middle powers. This sub-chapter explores the historical and geopolitical factors that contribute to these conflicts, delving into their impact on regional stability and global security. It also examines the role of diplomacy, negotiation, and international mediation in resolving territorial disputes among middle powers.

Political Rivalries and Power Struggles:

Political rivalries and power struggles are inherent in the interactions among regional middle powers. This sub-chapter analyzes the underlying causes of these rivalries, the strategies employed by middle powers to gain political influence, and the implications for regional stability. It also highlights the role of diplomatic channels and international organizations in managing and mitigating these conflicts.

Conclusion:

Understanding the antagonisms and jealousies among regional middle powers is crucial for diplomats, economists, and strategists alike. By comprehending the complex interplay of these dynamics, stakeholders can devise effective strategies to promote regional integration, cooperation, and peace. This sub-chapter provides a comprehensive overview of the diverse dimensions of middle power maneuvers, offering insights into their implications for global security and stability.

Chapter 4: Competition for Regional Influence Among Middle Powers

Drivers of competition among regional middle powers

In the complex web of global diplomacy and power dynamics, regional middle powers play a crucial role in shaping the geopolitical landscape. These middle powers, characterized by their significant regional influence and capabilities, are often driven by various factors that fuel competition among them. Understanding the drivers behind this competition is essential for diplomats, economists, and strategists seeking to navigate the intricacies of regional politics and power struggles. This subchapter explores the key drivers of competition among regional middle powers.

One of the primary drivers is the antagonisms or jealousies that exist between these middle powers. Historical rivalries, territorial disputes, and cultural clashes can fuel animosity and competition for influence. These antagonisms not only impact regional dynamics but also have broader implications for global diplomacy and power dynamics.

Economic rivalries and trade disputes further intensify competition among regional middle powers. As these powers seek to expand their economic influence, they engage in fierce competition for markets, resources, and investment opportunities. This economic rivalry often leads to trade disputes, protectionist measures, and even economic sanctions, which can have far-reaching consequences for regional stability and global trade.

Political rivalries and power struggles also play a significant role in driving competition among regional middle powers. As these powers vie for political dominance, they engage in power struggles, alliances, and counterbalancing strategies. These political rivalries can escalate tensions and create a volatile environment in the region.

Territorial disputes and conflicts are another driver of competition among regional middle powers. Disputes over land, maritime boundaries, and resources can escalate into conflicts, fueling competition for control and influence. These territorial disputes not only affect the stability of the region but can also have implications for global security and stability.

Moreover, the role of regional middle powers in regional integration and cooperation is another important driver of competition. These powers often vie for leadership roles in regional organizations and initiatives, seeking to shape the direction of regional integration. This competition for regional integration can either foster cooperation or exacerbate tensions among middle powers.

Lastly, energy resources play a crucial role in driving competition among regional middle powers. As the demand for energy resources continues to rise, these powers compete for access to and control over energy reserves. This competition can lead to geopolitical tensions, resource conflicts, and even military confrontations.

Understanding the drivers of competition among regional middle powers is essential for diplomats, economists, and strategists. By comprehending these dynamics, stakeholders can navigate the complexities of regional politics, anticipate conflicts, and work towards fostering stability, cooperation, and global security.

Strategies employed by middle powers to gain influence in their region

Title: Strategies Employed by Middle Powers to Gain Influence in Their Region

Introduction:

In the complex web of global diplomacy and power dynamics, middle powers play a crucial role in shaping regional politics and influencing global affairs. This subchapter explores the strategies employed by these middle powers to gain influence in their respective regions. From economic rivalries to security alliances, this analysis sheds light on the intricacies of middle power maneuvers and their implications on global security and stability.

Economic Rivalries and Trade Disputes:

Middle powers often engage in economic rivalries and trade disputes to establish their dominance in the region. By leveraging their economic prowess, these states employ strategies such as protectionism, tariff wars, and preferential trade agreements to advance their interests and gain influence over neighboring nations.

Territorial Disputes and Conflicts:

Territorial disputes and conflicts are another avenue through which middle powers seek to expand their influence. These powers employ diplomatic negotiations, international arbitration, and, in some cases, military force to secure control over contested territories, thereby strengthening their regional standing.

Political Rivalries and Power Struggles:

Political rivalries and power struggles are inherent in regional politics. Middle powers skillfully navigate these dynamics by forming alliances, engaging in diplomatic negotiations, and leveraging their political clout to gain influence in their region. These strategies allow them to shape regional policies and assert their interests.

Security Alliances and Counterbalancing Strategies:

Middle powers often form security alliances and employ counterbalancing strategies to safeguard their interests and maintain regional stability. By forging partnerships with other like-minded states, these powers can collectively counter the influence of larger global players, thus increasing their own regional leverage.

Cultural and Identity Clashes:

Cultural and identity clashes among regional middle powers pose unique challenges. To navigate these complexities, middle powers employ strategies such as cultural diplomacy, soft power initiatives, and regional integration efforts to bridge gaps and foster cooperation, ultimately enhancing their influence in the region.

Role in Regional Integration and Cooperation:

Middle powers recognize the importance of regional integration and cooperation. By actively participating in regional organizations, promoting economic partnerships, and fostering cultural exchanges, these states solidify their position as regional leaders and gain influence through collaborative efforts.

Energy Resources and Competition:

Energy resources play a crucial role in determining regional power dynamics. Middle powers employ strategies such as energy diplomacy, investment in energy infrastructure, and resource-sharing agreements to secure access to vital energy resources and gain influence over energy-rich regions.

Conclusion:

The strategies employed by middle powers to gain influence in their regions are diverse and multifaceted. The dynamics of economic rivalries, territorial disputes, political power struggles, security alliances, cultural clashes, and energy competitions all contribute to shaping the influence and impact of middle powers on global diplomacy and power dynamics. Understanding these strategies is essential for diplomats, economists, and strategists to navigate the complex world of middle power maneuvers and anticipate the implications of regional middle power conflicts on global security and stability.

Case studies: Competing for regional influence

In the world of international relations, the dynamics between regional middle powers have always been a fascinating subject. The antagonisms and jealousies that arise from their competition for regional influence can have a significant impact on global diplomacy and power dynamics. This subchapter explores various case studies that shed light on the complexities and nuances of this phenomenon.

One prominent case study is the rivalry between India and China in South Asia. These two regional powerhouses have been vying for influence in countries such as Nepal, Sri Lanka, and Bangladesh. Through economic investments, infrastructure projects, and diplomatic maneuvering, both India and China seek to secure their interests and expand their spheres of influence. The resulting economic rivalries and trade disputes have far-reaching implications for the region, as well as for global trade and investment patterns.

Another case study examines the territorial disputes and conflicts between Japan and South Korea in East Asia. Historical grievances and competing claims over islands have strained relations between these two regional middle powers. The political rivalries and power struggles that ensue not only affect their bilateral relations but also have implications for the broader security architecture in the region.

In the Middle East, the security alliances and counterbalancing strategies of Saudi Arabia and Iran illustrate the complex nature of regional power dynamics. The ongoing proxy conflicts in Yemen and Syria highlight the geopolitical struggle for dominance between these two regional powers. Their cultural and identity clashes further exacerbate the tensions, making it difficult to achieve regional integration and cooperation.

The competition for energy resources is also a significant factor in regional power rivalries. The case of Russia and Turkey in the Black Sea region exemplifies this. Both countries have competing interests in the energy-rich region, leading to heightened tensions and geopolitical maneuvering. The implications of such conflicts on global security and stability cannot be underestimated.

These case studies underscore the multifaceted nature of the antagonisms and jealousies among regional middle powers. Understanding the intricacies of their rivalries is crucial for diplomats, economists, and strategists alike. By analyzing these case studies, we can gain insights into the impact of regional middle powers on global diplomacy and power dynamics. Moreover, it enables us to identify potential avenues for regional integration, cooperation, and conflict resolution. In an increasingly interconnected world, where regional players have a significant role to play, comprehending the dynamics of their interactions is essential for maintaining peace and stability.

Sub-chapter heading

Sub-chapter heading: The Role of Regional Middle Powers in Regional Integration and Cooperation

In this sub-chapter, we will explore the significant role that regional middle powers play in fostering regional integration and cooperation. This topic is of utmost importance to diplomats, economists, and strategists who seek to understand the dynamics of regional power and its implications on global diplomacy.

Regional middle powers, with their unique geopolitical positions and relative influence, often find themselves at the center of regional integration efforts. Their ability to bridge gaps, mediate conflicts, and build consensus among neighboring countries is crucial in promoting stability and cooperation.

These middle powers have the potential to shape regional agendas, influence decision-making processes, and facilitate multilateral negotiations. Through their diplomatic engagement, they can create platforms for dialogue, address common challenges, and foster trust-building measures among regional actors.

The impact of regional middle powers on regional integration and cooperation extends beyond diplomatic efforts. Their economic strength and trade networks enable them to drive economic integration initiatives, promote regional trade, and facilitate the flow of goods, services, and investments. By leveraging their economic influence, these middle powers can incentivize cooperation among neighboring states and create a conducive environment for regional economic growth.

Furthermore, regional middle powers often form security alliances and counterbalancing strategies to enhance regional stability. By collaborating on matters of defense, intelligence sharing, and joint military exercises, these middle powers can deter aggression, prevent conflicts, and maintain a balance of power within the region. Such security alliances also promote trust and confidence-building among regional actors, contributing to regional stability and peace.

Cultural and identity clashes are common among regional middle powers, but they can also serve as a driving force for regional integration. By recognizing and respecting the cultural diversity within their regions, middle powers can facilitate dialogue and cooperation based on shared values and understanding. This inclusivity can lead to a stronger sense of regional identity and promote cooperation in various sectors, including education, tourism, and cultural exchange.

In conclusion, the role of regional middle powers in regional integration and cooperation cannot be underestimated. Their diplomatic efforts, economic influence, security alliances, and cultural understanding are essential in overcoming antagonisms and fostering cooperation among neighboring states. By understanding the dynamics of these middle powers and their impact on global diplomacy and power dynamics, diplomats, economists, and strategists can better navigate the complexities of regional politics and contribute to global security and stability.

Sub-chapter heading

Sub-chapter Heading: The Impact of Regional Middle Powers on Global Diplomacy and Power Dynamics

Regional middle powers play a crucial role in shaping global diplomacy and power dynamics. In this sub-chapter, we will delve into the various ways in which these middle powers influence and impact the international stage. Diplomats, economists, and strategists will gain valuable insights into the complexities of regional rivalries, economic disputes, and territorial conflicts, and how they shape the global order.

The antagonisms or jealousies of regional middle powers form the foundation of this discussion. As we explore the underlying motivations and historical contexts, readers will gain a deeper understanding of the intricate dynamics that drive these rivalries. By analyzing the economic rivalries and trade disputes among regional middle powers, we can assess how these competitions affect global trade and economic stability.

Territorial disputes and conflicts between regional middle powers often have far-reaching consequences on international relations. Through case studies and expert analysis, diplomats and strategists will gain insights into the root causes of these conflicts and potential pathways to resolution. Furthermore, the sub-chapter will shed light on the political rivalries and power struggles among regional middle powers, and how they impact regional stability and global diplomacy.

Security alliances and counterbalancing strategies are vital aspects of the middle powers' pursuit of regional influence. Diplomats and strategists will gain a comprehensive understanding of the various security alliances and counterbalancing strategies employed by these powers to safeguard their interests. Additionally, the sub-chapter will explore the cultural and identity clashes that often exacerbate tensions among regional middle powers, highlighting the need for cultural diplomacy and conflict resolution.

The role of regional middle powers in regional integration and cooperation is of paramount importance. Readers will gain insights into how these powers contribute to regional stability and foster cooperation in areas such as trade, security, and cultural exchange. Furthermore, the sub-chapter will explore the implications of regional middle power conflicts on global security and stability, providing strategists with a comprehensive understanding of the potential risks and challenges.

Overall, this sub-chapter aims to provide diplomats, economists, and strategists with a comprehensive analysis of the impact of regional middle powers on global diplomacy and power dynamics. By unraveling the antagonisms and jealousies of these players, we can better navigate the complex landscape of international relations and work towards a more stable and cooperative global order.

Chapter 5: Economic Rivalries and Trade Disputes Among Regional Middle Powers

Economic interdependencies among regional middle powers

Economic interdependencies among regional middle powers play a crucial role in shaping global diplomacy, power dynamics, and regional influence. In the subchapter titled "Economic interdependencies among regional middle powers," we delve into the intricacies of economic rivalries, trade disputes, and their impact on various aspects of international relations.

Regional middle powers often find themselves entangled in antagonisms and jealousies, driven by economic competition. These powers strive to assert their influence and secure advantageous positions in regional and global markets. By analyzing their economic interdependencies, we gain insights into their motivations, actions, and the resulting implications.

Trade disputes among regional middle powers can have far-reaching consequences. Economists, diplomats, and strategists need to understand the underlying factors behind these disputes and their potential effects on global security and stability. By examining case studies, we explore how such conflicts arise, escalate, and impact both regional and international trade.

Territorial disputes and conflicts between regional middle powers are often fueled by economic interests. These disputes not only jeopardize bilateral relations but also have wider implications for regional integration and cooperation. By studying the economic dimensions of these conflicts, diplomats and strategists can devise effective counterbalancing strategies and security alliances to maintain stability and prevent further escalation.

Political rivalries and power struggles among regional middle powers are closely intertwined with economic considerations. Understanding the economic motivations behind these rivalries helps in comprehending their dynamics and formulating effective diplomatic approaches. By analyzing the role of economic interdependencies, we shed light on the root causes of these disputes and explore potential avenues for resolution.

Cultural and identity clashes among regional middle powers also have economic dimensions. These clashes can impede regional integration and cooperation, hindering economic progress and stability. By exploring the influence of cultural and identity factors on economic interdependencies, diplomats and economists can identify areas of potential collaboration and bridge differences.

Furthermore, energy resources and competition among regional middle powers have significant implications for global energy security. By examining the economic interdependencies in the energy sector, strategists can assess the potential risks and devise strategies to mitigate them. Understanding the economic underpinnings of energy-related conflicts enables policymakers to promote cooperation and stability in this critical domain.

In conclusion, the subchapter on economic interdependencies among regional middle powers provides a comprehensive analysis of the complex dynamics at play. This content is essential for diplomats, economists, and strategists who seek to understand the multifaceted nature of regional rivalries, their impact on global diplomacy, power dynamics, and the implications for global security and stability.

Common trade disputes and their implications

Common trade disputes can have significant implications for regional middle powers and their relationships with other countries. These disputes often arise due to economic rivalries, different trade policies, or conflicting interests in specific industries. In this subchapter, we will explore some of the most common trade disputes among regional middle powers and analyze their implications on global diplomacy, power dynamics, and regional integration.

One of the most prevalent trade disputes among regional middle powers is the competition for regional influence. As these middle powers strive to expand their economic and political clout, they often engage in trade wars, tariff disputes, or unfair trade practices to gain a competitive advantage. These actions not only strain diplomatic relations but also create tensions in global power dynamics, as larger powers may get involved to protect their own interests.

Economic rivalries and trade disputes can also lead to territorial conflicts between regional middle powers. Disputes over valuable resources or strategic locations can escalate into full-fledged conflicts, threatening regional stability and security. Diplomats and strategists need to carefully navigate these disputes to prevent armed conflicts and find peaceful resolutions.

Political rivalries and power struggles among regional middle powers can also manifest in trade disputes. These middle powers may impose trade barriers or tariffs on each other as a means of exerting political pressure or gaining leverage. Such actions can have far-reaching consequences for global security and stability, as they may trigger a chain reaction of retaliatory measures and further strain diplomatic relations.

Furthermore, cultural and identity clashes among regional middle powers can exacerbate trade disputes. Differences in cultural norms, values, and business practices can lead to misunderstandings and conflicts, impeding trade relations and hindering regional integration efforts.

Energy resources often play a significant role in trade disputes among regional middle powers. The competition for valuable energy resources, such as oil, gas, or renewable energy sources, can intensify rivalries and increase the likelihood of conflicts. Diplomats and economists must find ways to mitigate these disputes and encourage cooperation in the sustainable development and distribution of energy resources.

In conclusion, trade disputes among regional middle powers have far-reaching implications for global security, stability, and diplomacy. They can strain diplomatic relations, trigger territorial conflicts, and disrupt regional integration efforts. Diplomats, economists, and strategists must closely monitor and navigate these disputes to maintain peaceful relations and foster mutually beneficial trade relationships among regional middle powers.

Sub-chapter heading

Sub-chapter Heading: The Impact of Regional Middle Powers on Global Diplomacy and Power Dynamics

In today's rapidly changing global landscape, regional middle powers have emerged as crucial players in shaping the course of international diplomacy and power dynamics. This sub-chapter explores the multifaceted impact of these middle powers on the global stage, delving into their contributions, challenges, and implications for the world order.

As diplomats, economists, and strategists delve into the intricacies of regional middle powers, it becomes evident that their antagonisms and jealousies play a significant role in shaping global dynamics. The competition for regional influence among these powers not only affects their immediate surroundings but also reverberates globally. This sub-chapter examines the factors driving such rivalries, including economic rivalries, trade disputes, territorial conflicts, and political power struggles, shedding light on their implications for the broader diplomatic landscape.

Moreover, this sub-chapter delves into the security alliances and counterbalancing strategies of regional middle powers, highlighting their efforts to safeguard their interests and maintain stability within their regions. Cultural and identity clashes among these powers also play a significant role in shaping their interactions and can have far-reaching consequences for regional integration and cooperation.

Given the increasing importance of energy resources, this sub-chapter also investigates the competition among regional middle powers for control over these vital assets. It explores the implications of such rivalries on global energy security and analyzes strategies employed by these powers to secure their access to energy resources.

Lastly, this sub-chapter addresses the implications of regional middle power conflicts on global security and stability. The ongoing tensions and rivalries among these powers have the potential to create ripple effects that transcend regional boundaries, posing challenges to global actors and institutions.

By unraveling the antagonisms and jealousies of regional middle powers, this sub-chapter aims to provide diplomats, economists, and strategists with a comprehensive understanding of the impact of these powers on global diplomacy and power dynamics. It emphasizes the need for effective engagement and cooperation between these powers to ensure a stable, secure, and prosperous world order.

Sub-chapter heading

Sub-chapter Heading: The Impact of Regional Middle Powers on Global Diplomacy and Power Dynamics

In this sub-chapter, we will delve into the significant influence that regional middle powers hold in shaping global diplomacy and power dynamics. By examining their actions, motivations, and strategies, we can gain a deeper understanding of the antagonisms and jealousies that arise among these players.

Regional middle powers, often located in geographically strategic locations, have emerged as key actors in the global arena. Their actions, whether intentional or unintentional, can have far-reaching consequences that impact the balance of power and shape the international order.

One of the most significant aspects to explore is the competition for regional influence among middle powers. As these countries strive to expand their spheres of influence, tensions and rivalries can arise, leading to complex diplomatic maneuvers and power struggles. We will analyze specific case studies, such as the rivalry between India and China in South Asia or the competition between Brazil and Argentina in South America, to understand how these dynamics play out.

Economic rivalries and trade disputes also play a crucial role in the antagonisms among regional middle powers. With economic growth and prosperity at stake, these countries often engage in intense competition for resources, markets, and investment opportunities. Examining the economic dimensions of these conflicts will provide insights into the strategies employed by middle powers to gain an economic advantage.

Furthermore, territorial disputes and conflicts between regional middle powers have the potential to escalate into serious crises with global implications. We will examine the historical and ongoing conflicts, such as the South China Sea disputes or the tensions in the Korean Peninsula, to understand the underlying factors driving these conflicts and their impact on regional and global stability.

Political rivalries and power struggles among regional middle powers also shape the landscape of international relations. By analyzing the dynamics of these rivalries, we can uncover the motivations behind their actions and the strategies they adopt to gain political influence and power.

Security alliances and counterbalancing strategies pursued by regional middle powers will be explored to understand how these countries navigate the complex web of international relations. We will examine case studies, like the ASEAN regional forum or the BRICS alliance, to examine the motivations, challenges, and implications of these security alliances.

The clash of cultures and identities among regional middle powers is another important dimension to consider. By exploring the cultural and identity factors that shape their interactions, we can gain insights into the root causes of conflicts and tensions.

Lastly, we will examine the role of regional middle powers in regional integration and cooperation efforts. These countries often play a vital role in facilitating regional cooperation and integration, acting as intermediaries or mediators in conflicts.

Overall, this sub-chapter aims to unravel the complex web of antagonisms and jealousies among regional middle powers and shed light on their impact on global diplomacy and power dynamics. By understanding these dynamics, diplomats, economists, and strategists can navigate the intricate world of international relations more effectively and contribute to global security and stability.

Chapter 6: Territorial Disputes and Conflicts Between Regional Middle Powers

Historical background of territorial disputes among regional middle powers

Territorial disputes have long been a source of tension and conflicts among regional middle powers, shaping the dynamics of global diplomacy and power struggles. Understanding the historical background of these disputes provides crucial insights into the antagonisms and jealousies that exist among these players.

Throughout history, regional middle powers have consistently sought to expand their influence and control over strategic territories, often leading to clashes with neighboring states. These disputes can be traced back to the colonial era when European powers carved up territories in regions such as Asia, Africa, and the Middle East, leading to the creation of artificial borders that have remained contentious to this day.

One notable example is the territorial disputes in the South China Sea, involving countries like China, Vietnam, the Philippines, and Malaysia. These conflicts stem from historical claims and territorial ambitions, exacerbated by the abundance of natural resources and strategic maritime routes in the area. The struggle for control over these territories has led to heightened tensions and a complex web of alliances and counterbalancing strategies among regional middle powers.

Similarly, in the Middle East, the Israeli-Palestinian conflict has been a longstanding territorial dispute with far-reaching implications. The competing claims over land and resources have fueled political rivalries, security alliances, and cultural clashes among regional middle powers.

The impact of this conflict extends beyond the region, affecting global security and stability.

Economic rivalries and trade disputes also play a significant role in territorial conflicts among regional middle powers. Resource-rich regions like Central Asia, Africa, and Latin America often become battlegrounds for these powers seeking to secure access to valuable commodities. Competition for regional influence and control over energy resources has driven conflicts and shaped the balance of power in these regions.

As diplomats, economists, and strategists, it is essential to recognize the historical context of territorial disputes among regional middle powers. By understanding the root causes and dynamics of these conflicts, we can better analyze their impact on global diplomacy, power dynamics, and regional integration. Furthermore, recognizing the implications of these conflicts on global security and stability allows us to develop effective strategies for conflict resolution and cooperation among these regional players.

Case studies: Ongoing territorial conflicts

Territorial disputes among regional middle powers have long been a source of tension and conflict, impacting global diplomacy, power dynamics, and regional stability. This subchapter explores several case studies that shed light on the complexities and challenges of these ongoing conflicts.

One such case study is the ongoing dispute between India and Pakistan over the region of Kashmir. This territorial conflict, rooted in historical, political, and cultural differences, has resulted in multiple wars and continues to strain relations between the two nuclear-armed nations. The implications of this conflict are significant, not only for regional stability but also for global security, as it has the potential to escalate into a larger-scale conflict.

Another case study that exemplifies the impact of territorial disputes among regional middle powers is the South China Sea conflict. China's assertive territorial claims and its aggressive actions in the disputed waters have raised tensions with neighboring countries such as Vietnam, the Philippines, and Malaysia. These disputes have wide-ranging implications, not only for the countries involved but also for the broader region and global power dynamics, as major powers like the United States seek to counterbalance Chinese influence.

The Middle East provides another fertile ground for territorial conflicts among regional middle powers. The Israeli-Palestinian conflict, for instance, has deep historical and religious roots and has remained unresolved for decades. The ongoing dispute over land and self-determination has ramifications beyond the region, shaping global diplomacy and fueling tensions between different factions and countries.

These case studies illustrate the multidimensional nature of ongoing territorial conflicts among regional middle powers. They highlight the economic, political, cultural, and security dimensions at play, as well as the potential for these conflicts to escalate and impact global stability.

Understanding and analyzing these conflicts is crucial for diplomats, economists, and strategists, as they navigate the complex web of antagonisms and jealousies among regional middle powers. By examining the causes, dynamics, and implications of these conflicts, policymakers can develop strategies to mitigate tensions, promote regional integration and cooperation, and maintain global security.

In conclusion, ongoing territorial conflicts among regional middle powers have far-reaching consequences, affecting not only the countries directly involved but also the broader international community. By studying these conflicts, diplomats, economists, and strategists can gain valuable insights into the intricacies of regional power dynamics and work towards peaceful resolutions that promote stability and cooperation.

Sub-chapter heading

Sub-chapter Heading: The Impact of Regional Middle Powers on Global Diplomacy and Power Dynamics

In the complex landscape of international relations, regional middle powers play a significant role in shaping global diplomacy and power dynamics. These middle powers, characterized by their economic and political influence within their respective regions, often find themselves entangled in antagonisms and jealousies that have far-reaching consequences for the international community. This sub-chapter delves into the multifaceted dimensions of their impact and provides insights into the various dynamics at play.

One of the key aspects explored in this sub-chapter is the competition for regional influence among middle powers. As these states strive to expand their spheres of influence, they engage in economic rivalries and trade disputes that have both regional and global implications. Through their economic prowess, these middle powers seek to solidify their positions and gain leverage in international negotiations.

Territorial disputes and conflicts between regional middle powers also feature prominently in this sub-chapter. These conflicts, driven by political rivalries and power struggles, not only have immediate consequences for the involved parties but also pose significant challenges to global security and stability. The sub-chapter analyzes the strategies employed by middle powers to counterbalance their rivals and form security alliances, shedding light on the intricate interplay between regional and global interests.

Furthermore, cultural and identity clashes among regional middle powers are explored in this sub-chapter. These clashes, rooted in historical grievances and differing ideologies, impede regional integration and cooperation. The sub-chapter examines the role of middle powers in fostering regional unity and the potential implications of these cultural divisions on global security.

Another crucial aspect discussed is the role of middle powers in energy resource competition. As these states vie for control over energy resources, regional power dynamics are further complicated, potentially leading to conflicts that transcend national borders. The sub-chapter investigates the implications of these rivalries not only on regional stability but also on global energy security.

In conclusion, this sub-chapter highlights the significant impact of regional middle powers on global diplomacy and power dynamics. By examining the antagonisms, economic rivalries, territorial disputes, political rivalries, security alliances, cultural clashes, energy resource competition, and their implications on regional integration and global security, diplomats, economists, and strategists can gain valuable insights into the intricate dynamics of these middle powers. Understanding these dynamics is crucial for navigating the complexities of international relations and promoting global stability.

Sub-chapter heading

Sub-chapter Heading: The Impact of Regional Middle Powers on Global Diplomacy and Power Dynamics

In the complex web of international relations, regional middle powers play a significant role in shaping global diplomacy and power dynamics. This sub-chapter delves into the multifaceted impact of these middle powers, addressing their antagonisms, jealousies, and their influence on various aspects of the global stage.

At the heart of regional middle power dynamics lies a delicate balance of competition and cooperation. The rivalry among these powers for regional influence is an ever-present force, driving them to pursue economic advantages, trade disputes, and territorial conflicts. Diplomats, economists, and strategists must closely examine these antagonisms to navigate the intricate web of regional power struggles.

However, it is essential to recognize that the impact of regional middle powers extends far beyond their immediate spheres of influence. Their actions have repercussions on global security and stability. As middle powers forge security alliances and employ counterbalancing strategies, the balance of power at the international level subtly shifts. Understanding these alliances and their implications is vital for diplomats and strategists seeking to maintain global stability.

Cultural and identity clashes among regional middle powers are yet another dimension to consider. These clashes play a significant role in shaping regional integration and cooperation efforts. Diplomats must be well-versed in the historical, cultural, and religious nuances that underpin these conflicts in order to navigate delicate negotiations and foster regional unity.

Economic rivalries, particularly in the realm of energy resources, heighten the stakes for regional middle powers. The competition for limited resources can strain diplomatic relations and exacerbate conflicts. By analyzing the implications of these rivalries, economists can predict potential disruptions to global energy markets and strategists can develop contingency plans to mitigate tensions.

The influence of regional middle powers on global diplomacy and power dynamics cannot be understated. As diplomats, economists, and strategists, understanding these dynamics is crucial for navigating the complex world of international relations. By studying the antagonisms, economic rivalries, territorial conflicts, and cultural clashes among regional middle powers, professionals can develop informed strategies that promote regional integration, cooperation, and ultimately, global security and stability.

Chapter 7: Political Rivalries and Power Struggles Among Regional Middle Powers

Competing ideologies and political systems among regional middle powers

In the modern geopolitical landscape, regional middle powers have emerged as significant players, exerting their influence on global diplomacy and power dynamics. These middle powers, with their varying ideologies and political systems, often find themselves locked in fierce competition for regional influence. This subchapter aims to unravel the antagonisms and jealousies that arise among these regional middle powers due to their differing ideologies.

The impact of regional middle powers on global diplomacy and power dynamics cannot be understated. As diplomats, economists, and strategists, it is crucial for us to understand the intricate dynamics that shape the relationships between these middle powers. Their ideological differences often become the driving force behind their actions and decisions in the international arena.

The competition for regional influence among middle powers can manifest in various forms. Economic rivalries and trade disputes are common occurrences as these powers vie for dominance in regional markets. Territorial disputes and conflicts also arise, further exacerbating tensions between them. Political rivalries and power struggles add another layer of complexity to these relationships, as middle powers seek to establish their supremacy within the region.

Security alliances and counterbalancing strategies play a significant role in the power dynamics of regional middle powers. These alliances are often formed to counter the influence of rival powers and protect their own interests. However, cultural and identity clashes can complicate these alliances, as differing ideologies and values come into play.

The role of regional middle powers in regional integration and cooperation cannot be overlooked. Their actions and policies can either foster cooperation or hinder progress in regional integration efforts. Additionally, the competition for energy resources among these middle powers further intensifies the rivalries and adds another dimension to the power struggles.

The implications of conflicts and tensions among regional middle powers extend beyond their immediate regions. These conflicts can have far-reaching consequences for global security and stability. As diplomats, economists, and strategists, it is essential for us to analyze and understand these conflicts to develop effective strategies for maintaining global peace and stability.

In conclusion, the competing ideologies and political systems among regional middle powers give rise to antagonisms and jealousies that shape global diplomacy and power dynamics. The economic, territorial, political, and cultural rivalries among these powers have significant implications for regional integration, energy competition, and global security. It is imperative for diplomats, economists, and strategists to study and comprehend these dynamics in order to navigate the complexities of international relations successfully.

Power struggles within regional organizations

Regional organizations play a crucial role in shaping the dynamics of global diplomacy and power relations. However, behind the façade of cooperation and integration, power struggles often simmer among the middle powers within these organizations. In this subchapter, we will delve into the various dimensions of these power struggles, exploring their implications for global security, stability, and economic development.

One of the primary causes of power struggles among regional middle powers is the antagonism and jealousy that stems from their quest for influence. As these states vie for regional dominance, they engage in a complex web of political rivalries and power struggles. These competitions often manifest in economic rivalries and trade disputes, as middle powers seek to secure economic advantages and protect their national interests.

Territorial disputes and conflicts are another source of power struggles within regional organizations. Middle powers frequently find themselves entangled in territorial disputes with their neighbors, leading to heightened tensions and conflicts. These disputes not only threaten regional stability but also have significant implications for global security, as they can draw in major powers and disrupt the delicate balance of power.

In their pursuit of security and influence, middle powers form security alliances and employ counterbalancing strategies. These alliances serve as a means to counter the dominance of larger powers and ensure their own regional interests. However, such alliances can also exacerbate existing power struggles and create further divisions within regional organizations.

Cultural and identity clashes also contribute to power struggles among regional middle powers. Differences in political systems, ideologies, and historical narratives often fuel tensions and hinder cooperation. These clashes can impede regional integration and cooperation, preventing the collective efforts of regional organizations from achieving their full potential.

Furthermore, the competition for energy resources has emerged as a critical factor in power struggles among middle powers. As the demand for energy resources grows, regional middle powers compete to secure access to these valuable commodities, leading to increased tensions and rivalries.

The implications of these power struggles extend beyond regional boundaries. Conflicts among middle powers can have far-reaching consequences for global security and stability. The disruption of regional organizations and the breakdown of diplomatic relations can create power vacuums, exacerbate existing conflicts, and undermine international efforts to promote peace and cooperation.

In conclusion, power struggles within regional organizations are complex and multifaceted. They involve economic rivalries, territorial disputes, political rivalries, security alliances, cultural clashes, and energy competition. These struggles not only impact regional dynamics but also have far-reaching implications for global diplomacy, power relations, and the overall security and stability of the international system. Understanding and managing these power struggles is crucial for diplomats, economists, and strategists seeking to navigate the intricate web of regional middle power dynamics.

Sub-chapter heading

Sub-chapter Heading: Role of Regional Middle Powers in Regional Integration and Cooperation

In today's complex global landscape, regional middle powers have emerged as key players in shaping regional integration and cooperation. This sub-chapter delves into the pivotal role these middle powers play in fostering collaboration, resolving conflicts, and driving progress within their respective regions. Addressing the interests of diplomats, economists, and strategists, this section explores the multifaceted dynamics of regional integration and cooperation facilitated by middle powers.

One of the most significant contributions made by regional middle powers is their ability to bridge the gaps between larger global powers and smaller states within their region. By leveraging their diplomatic prowess and economic influence, middle powers act as mediators, bringing diverse nations together to foster dialogue, negotiate agreements, and build consensus. This role is crucial in overcoming the antagonisms and jealousies that often hinder cooperation among regional players.

Moreover, the impact of regional middle powers on global diplomacy and power dynamics cannot be overlooked. As they navigate the international stage, these middle powers often find themselves caught between the interests of major global players. Their strategic maneuvering and ability to balance competing influences make them vital actors in shaping the global order. Their actions can either amplify or mitigate tensions, ultimately impacting global security and stability.

Competition for regional influence among middle powers is another aspect that warrants attention. Economic rivalries and trade disputes often arise as middle powers strive to expand their spheres of influence. This sub-chapter analyzes the consequences of such rivalries, exploring their impact on regional integration efforts and the larger global economic landscape. By examining territorial disputes, political rivalries, and power struggles among regional middle powers, this section uncovers the underlying factors that shape their often complex relationships.

Security alliances and counterbalancing strategies adopted by regional middle powers also play a pivotal role in shaping regional dynamics. This sub-chapter delves into the intricacies of these alliances, the motivations behind them, and their impact on regional security.

Additionally, it explores the cultural and identity clashes that can arise among middle powers, shedding light on the potential obstacles to regional integration and collaboration.

Energy resources and competition among regional middle powers are also explored in this sub-chapter, as their access to and control over vital resources can significantly influence regional power dynamics. Finally, the implications of regional middle power conflicts on global security and stability are examined, emphasizing the interconnectedness of regional and global challenges.

This sub-chapter provides a comprehensive analysis of the role played by regional middle powers in regional integration and cooperation. By understanding their motivations, strategies, and impact, diplomats, economists, and strategists can gain valuable insights into the complexities of the global landscape and develop effective approaches to address the antagonisms and jealousies that can hinder progress.

Sub-chapter heading

Sub-chapter Heading: The Impact of Regional Middle Powers on Global Diplomacy and Power Dynamics

In this sub-chapter, we delve into the intricacies of how regional middle powers exert their influence on global diplomacy and power dynamics. As diplomats, economists, and strategists, understanding the role and actions of these regional players is crucial for comprehending the complexities of international relations.

The antagonisms or jealousies of regional middle powers are significant factors shaping global diplomacy. We explore the historical rivalries, territorial disputes, and political power struggles among these middle powers, shedding light on how these tensions impact the larger geopolitical landscape. By analyzing the drivers of these antagonisms, we can better predict and manage potential conflicts.

Moreover, the competition for regional influence among middle powers has far-reaching consequences. We examine the economic rivalries and trade disputes that emerge as these nations strive to establish themselves as dominant players in their respective regions. We also delve into the strategies employed by these middle powers to secure their influence, including forming security alliances and pursuing counterbalancing strategies.

Cultural and identity clashes among regional middle powers are another crucial aspect of their impact on global diplomacy. We investigate how these clashes shape regional integration and cooperation efforts, as well as the challenges they pose to achieving stability and peace. Understanding the dynamics of these clashes is essential for diplomats and strategists seeking to foster harmony and collaboration among regional powers.

Another key area of analysis is the role of regional middle powers in energy resources and competition. We explore the implications of their struggles for control over vital energy resources, as well as how these competitions affect global energy security. By examining the economic and strategic interests at play, we can gain insights into the motivations and actions of these middle powers.

Lastly, we discuss the broader implications of conflicts among regional middle powers on global security and stability. As strategists, it is crucial to assess the potential ripple effects of these conflicts and develop effective strategies to mitigate them. This sub-chapter provides a comprehensive understanding of the multifaceted dynamics between regional middle powers and their impact on the global stage.

By unraveling the antagonisms and jealousies of regional middle powers, diplomats, economists, and strategists can navigate the complex web of global diplomacy with greater nuance and foresight.

Chapter 8: Security Alliances and Counterbalancing Strategies of Regional Middle Powers

Importance of security alliances for regional middle powers

In the ever-evolving landscape of global diplomacy and power dynamics, regional middle powers play a crucial role in shaping the geopolitical arena. These middle powers, often situated in strategic locations and possessing significant economic and military capabilities, find themselves at the center of various antagonisms and jealousies. To navigate these challenges and exert influence on a global scale, forming security alliances becomes paramount.

Security alliances serve as a cornerstone for regional middle powers in their pursuit of stability, security, and influence. By forging partnerships with like-minded nations, middle powers can leverage their collective strength to counterbalance the dominance of major powers and protect their interests. Such alliances provide a platform for diplomatic, economic, and military collaboration, enabling regional middle powers to amplify their voices and increase their negotiating power.

Competition for regional influence among middle powers is a common feature of international politics. Security alliances offer a means for middle powers to consolidate their regional standing and enhance their collective weight. By aligning their interests, middle powers can leverage their combined resources to influence regional affairs, mediate conflicts, and promote regional integration and cooperation. This not only enhances their individual security but also contributes to global peace and stability.

Economic rivalries and trade disputes are often prevalent among regional middle powers. Security alliances can help mitigate these tensions by fostering economic cooperation, trade agreements, and dispute resolution mechanisms. By pooling their resources, middle powers can create a more favorable environment for trade and investment, spur economic growth, and overcome barriers that impede regional integration.

Furthermore, territorial disputes, political rivalries, and power struggles are common among regional middle powers. Security alliances provide a platform for dialogue, confidence-building measures, and conflict resolution mechanisms. By cooperating on security matters, middle powers can reduce tensions, prevent conflicts from escalating, and establish mechanisms for peaceful resolution of disputes.

Security alliances also play a crucial role in countering cultural and identity clashes among regional middle powers. By fostering mutual understanding, respect, and cooperation, these alliances can bridge cultural divides and promote shared values. This not only strengthens regional integration but also enhances the global image and influence of middle powers.

In conclusion, security alliances are vital for regional middle powers in navigating the antagonisms, jealousies, and conflicts that characterize the global diplomatic landscape. These alliances provide a platform for collaboration, negotiation, and conflict resolution, enabling middle powers to protect their interests, exert influence, and contribute to regional stability and global security. By forging strong and strategic partnerships, regional middle powers can overcome the challenges they face and play a significant role in shaping the future of international relations.

Case studies: Regional security alliances and counterbalancing strategies

In the ever-evolving landscape of global diplomacy and power dynamics, regional middle powers play a crucial role in shaping the course of international relations. These middle powers, often situated in strategic geographical locations, are characterized by their economic prowess, political influence, and regional clout. Understanding the intricacies of their interactions, specifically in terms of security alliances and counterbalancing strategies, is essential for diplomats, economists, and strategists alike.

One notable case study is the antagonisms or jealousies of regional middle powers. These powers, driven by their aspirations for regional dominance, often clash over economic rivalries, trade disputes, territorial conflicts, and political power struggles. The impact of these tensions on global diplomacy and power dynamics cannot be underestimated, as they have the potential to disrupt regional integration and cooperation.

Competition for regional influence among middle powers is another crucial aspect to consider. Middle powers, such as Brazil, India, and South Africa, vie for regional hegemony, employing a range of strategies to enhance their standing. This competition can lead to both cooperation and conflict, with implications for global security and stability.

Security alliances and counterbalancing strategies are employed by regional middle powers to safeguard their interests and maintain regional stability. For instance, the Association of Southeast Asian Nations (ASEAN) has served as a platform for security cooperation among its member states, promoting dialogue and conflict resolution. Similarly, the Shanghai Cooperation Organization (SCO) has emerged as a counterbalancing force to Western influence, particularly in Central Asia.

Territorial disputes and conflicts between regional middle powers also deserve attention. The South China Sea dispute between China and several Southeast Asian nations, for example, has escalated tensions and raised concerns about the potential for conflict in the region. Understanding these territorial disputes and their implications is crucial for diplomats and strategists tasked with maintaining peace and stability.

Cultural and identity clashes among regional middle powers further complicate the dynamics of regional politics. Differences in religion, language, and historical grievances can contribute to tensions and rivalries, which must be carefully managed to avoid further escalation.

Lastly, the role of regional middle powers in regional integration and cooperation cannot be overlooked. These powers often act as catalysts for economic development, trade, and investment, driving regional integration initiatives such as the Pacific Alliance and the Gulf Cooperation Council. Their contributions to regional cooperation have implications not only for their respective regions but also for global economic stability and growth.

In conclusion, the study of regional security alliances and counterbalancing strategies among middle powers is of utmost importance for diplomats, economists, and strategists. The antagonisms, rivalries, and conflicts that arise between these powers have far-reaching implications for global diplomacy, power dynamics, and security. By understanding and analyzing these case studies, we can gain valuable insights into the complex dynamics of regional politics and work towards a more stable and cooperative world order.

Sub-chapter heading

Sub-chapter heading: The Impact of Regional Middle Powers on Global Diplomacy and Power Dynamics

In today's complex and interconnected world, middle powers play a pivotal role in shaping global diplomacy and power dynamics. These regional players, situated between great powers and smaller states, exert significant influence through their unique capabilities and strategic maneuvering. This sub-chapter delves into the various ways in which the antagonisms and jealousies of regional middle powers impact global diplomacy and power dynamics, shedding light on the complexities of their interactions.

Middle powers are not just passive spectators in the international arena; they actively engage in competition for regional influence, often clashing with one another over economic rivalries, trade disputes, territorial conflicts, and political power struggles. Their actions reverberate far beyond their immediate regions, impacting global security and stability. By examining these dynamics, diplomats, economists, and strategists can gain valuable insights into the key factors driving these conflicts and the implications they have on the global stage.

One critical aspect of regional middle power dynamics is the formation of security alliances and counterbalancing strategies. As middle powers seek to protect their interests and assert their influence, they often forge alliances with like-minded states to counter the dominance of larger powers. These alliances have far-reaching consequences, shaping the balance of power and influencing the outcomes of global conflicts and crises.

Cultural and identity clashes among regional middle powers also contribute to the complexities of global diplomacy. These conflicts, rooted in historical grievances and differing ideologies, can escalate tensions and hinder regional integration and cooperation.

Understanding these cultural dynamics is crucial for diplomats and strategists aiming to facilitate dialogue and find peaceful resolutions to conflicts.

Furthermore, the competition for energy resources among regional middle powers has emerged as a key driver of geopolitical rivalries. As energy demands rise, these middle powers vie for control over vital resources, leading to increased tensions and potential conflicts. This sub-chapter explores the implications of these rivalries on global energy security and the stability of the international system.

By unraveling the antagonisms and jealousies of regional middle powers, this sub-chapter provides diplomats, economists, and strategists with a comprehensive understanding of their impact on global diplomacy and power dynamics. Armed with this knowledge, stakeholders can devise informed policies and strategies that promote cooperation, mitigate conflicts, and foster stability in an increasingly multipolar world.

Sub-chapter heading

Sub-chapter heading: Understanding the Antagonisms and Jealousies of Regional Middle Powers

In this sub-chapter, we delve into the complex dynamics of regional middle powers and explore the underlying causes of their antagonisms and jealousies. Addressed to diplomats, economists, and strategists, this section aims to shed light on the various factors that contribute to conflicts and rivalries among these influential players on the global stage.

One of the key aspects we examine is the impact of regional middle powers on global diplomacy and power dynamics. These players often hold significant influence within their respective regions and their actions can shape the balance of power on a global scale. By studying their behavior, we can gain insights into the strategies they employ to maintain or enhance their regional influence.

Competition for regional influence among middle powers is another critical factor explored in this sub-chapter. Economic rivalries and trade disputes often arise as these powers vie for dominance in their shared regional markets. We delve into specific case studies to analyze the consequences of such rivalries and their implications for global economic stability.

Territorial disputes and conflicts between regional middle powers are also examined in detail. These conflicts can arise due to historical, cultural, or geopolitical factors, and have the potential to destabilize entire regions. By understanding the root causes of these disputes, diplomats and strategists can develop effective conflict resolution strategies.

Political rivalries and power struggles among regional middle powers are closely related to territorial disputes. We explore the intricate web of alliances and counterbalancing strategies employed by these players to gain an upper hand in their power struggles. Furthermore, cultural and identity clashes among regional middle powers are also discussed, as these often contribute to the deep-seated tensions between these nations.

The role of regional middle powers in regional integration and cooperation is an essential aspect covered in this sub-chapter. Despite their conflicts, these players also have the potential to contribute to regional stability and cooperation. Understanding their motivations and interests can pave the way for effective diplomatic engagements.

Lastly, we analyze the implications of regional middle power conflicts on global security and stability. As these conflicts have the potential to escalate and draw in other major powers, it is crucial to examine their impact on the broader international system.

By delving into these various facets, this sub-chapter provides a comprehensive understanding of the antagonisms and jealousies of regional middle powers. Diplomats, economists, and strategists can gain valuable insights into the complex dynamics at play and develop informed strategies to navigate and mitigate potential conflicts.

Chapter 9: Cultural and Identity Clashes Among Regional Middle Powers

Cultural diversity among regional middle powers

In the complex world of global diplomacy and power dynamics, the significance of regional middle powers cannot be underestimated. These nations, situated between major global players and smaller states, often find themselves caught in the crossfire of rivalries and competition. However, one aspect that adds a unique dimension to their interactions is the cultural diversity among these regional middle powers.

The antagonisms or jealousies of regional middle powers are often rooted in their distinct cultural identities. From language to religion, customs to traditions, these nations showcase a rich tapestry of diversity. Diplomats, economists, and strategists need to understand the impact of this cultural diversity on regional dynamics and how it shapes their interactions on the global stage.

Cultural diversity plays a crucial role in the competition for regional influence among middle powers. Each nation seeks to promote its unique cultural heritage and attract regional allies and partners. However, along with economic rivalries and trade disputes, cultural differences can create barriers to cooperation and hinder progress in regional integration and cooperation.

Territorial disputes and conflicts between regional middle powers are often fueled by cultural and identity clashes. Historical animosities, ethnic tensions, and divergent cultural narratives can exacerbate these conflicts, making them more challenging to resolve. Diplomats and strategists must navigate these complexities and find ways to bridge cultural divides to promote peace and stability in the region.

The role of regional middle powers in regional integration and cooperation is also influenced by cultural diversity. These nations often act as mediators and facilitators, using their cultural knowledge and understanding to bridge gaps and foster dialogue. Their ability to navigate cultural sensitivities and find common ground is crucial in promoting regional cohesion.

Furthermore, energy resources and competition among regional middle powers are deeply intertwined with cultural diversity. Access to and control over energy resources can be a source of tension and conflict. Cultural differences can exacerbate these rivalries as each nation seeks to secure its energy needs and assert its cultural influence in the region.

The implications of regional middle power conflicts on global security and stability cannot be ignored. As these nations engage in power struggles and security alliances, their cultural diversity can either be a source of strength or a vulnerability. Understanding the nuances of cultural dynamics is essential for diplomats, economists, and strategists to develop effective counterbalancing strategies and promote global peace.

In conclusion, cultural diversity among regional middle powers is a crucial factor that shapes their interactions in various dimensions. From economic rivalries to territorial conflicts, cultural and identity clashes to energy competition, understanding the impact of cultural diversity is vital for diplomats, economists, and strategists. By embracing these differences and finding common ground, regional middle powers can play a significant role in promoting regional integration, cooperation, and global stability.

Impact of cultural clashes on regional relations

The Impact of Cultural Clashes on Regional Relations

Culture plays a significant role in shaping the relationships between regional middle powers. The clash of cultures, values, and identities often leads to antagonisms and jealousies among these powers, influencing their actions and strategies on both regional and global platforms. Understanding the impact of cultural clashes on regional relations is crucial for diplomats, economists, and strategists, as it provides insights into the dynamics of power and influence in a given region.

Cultural clashes can arise from various sources, including historical grievances, religious differences, and ethnic rivalries. These clashes often lead to deep-rooted antagonisms and resentments, which can manifest in political rivalries, territorial disputes, and even armed conflicts between regional middle powers.

In the realm of global diplomacy, cultural clashes among regional middle powers can significantly impact power dynamics. These clashes often fuel competition for regional influence, as middle powers seek to assert their cultural values and identity on a broader stage. This competition can lead to economic rivalries and trade disputes, with each power vying for dominance in the regional market.

Security alliances and counterbalancing strategies are also influenced by cultural clashes among regional middle powers. Powers with similar cultural backgrounds may align themselves against those with different cultural orientations, leading to the formation of blocs and alliances that further multiply the complexities of regional relations.

Furthermore, cultural clashes have implications for regional integration and cooperation. Middle powers with divergent cultural values may find it challenging to collaborate on issues such as economic integration, security cooperation, and cultural exchanges. These clashes hinder progress towards regional integration and can impede efforts to foster cooperation and mutual understanding among regional middle powers.

Additionally, cultural clashes have implications for energy resources and competition among regional middle powers. Resources such as oil, gas, and minerals often become subject to intense competition, as middle powers seek to secure their energy needs and gain a competitive edge. This competition can exacerbate existing cultural tensions and further strain regional relations.

Ultimately, the impact of cultural clashes on regional relations extends beyond the regional arena. Conflicts and tensions among regional middle powers can have significant implications for global security and stability. The ripple effects of these clashes can be felt in global diplomatic efforts and power struggles among major players.

To navigate the intricacies of regional relations, diplomats, economists, and strategists must recognize the role of cultural clashes in shaping the behavior of regional middle powers. By understanding the impact of cultural clashes, they can develop strategies and policies that promote dialogue, cooperation, and peaceful resolution of conflicts among these powers. Only through such efforts can regional and global stability be ensured in an increasingly interconnected world.

Sub-chapter heading

Sub-chapter Heading: The Impact of Regional Middle Powers on Global Diplomacy and Power Dynamics

In today's rapidly evolving global landscape, the role of regional middle powers has become increasingly significant in shaping international relations. These regional players, characterized by their moderate power and influence, are often overlooked in discussions surrounding global diplomacy and power dynamics. However, the antagonisms and jealousies that arise among these middle powers have far-reaching implications, both regionally and globally.

The competition for regional influence among middle powers is a dynamic that cannot be ignored. As these countries strive to assert their dominance within their respective regions, their actions and strategies have a direct impact on global diplomacy. Their ability to form alliances and counterbalancing strategies can either stabilize or disrupt the existing power dynamics. The alliances formed by these middle powers often challenge the dominance of major powers, leading to a reconfiguration of global power structures.

Economic rivalries and trade disputes among regional middle powers further contribute to the complex web of global diplomacy. As these countries seek to secure their economic interests and gain a competitive edge, tensions can arise, leading to trade disputes and protectionist policies. Such conflicts not only disrupt regional stability but also have far-reaching consequences for global trade and economic growth.

Territorial disputes and conflicts between regional middle powers pose yet another challenge to global security and stability. These conflicts, rooted in historical grievances and competing claims, have the potential to escalate into full-blown military confrontations. The involvement of external powers in these disputes further complicates the situation, as their strategic interests often align with one side or the other.

Political rivalries and power struggles among regional middle powers have a direct impact on regional integration and cooperation efforts. These power struggles hinder cohesive decision-making and can derail attempts to foster regional unity. The clash of political ideologies and competing visions of regional integration can prevent middle powers from effectively addressing common challenges and pursuing shared goals.

Cultural and identity clashes among regional middle powers also play a significant role in shaping global diplomacy. These clashes, rooted in historical, religious, or ethnic differences, can fuel conflicts and hinder cooperation efforts. The failure to address cultural and identity issues can perpetuate animosities and prevent the formation of meaningful alliances.

Moreover, the role of regional middle powers in managing energy resources and the competition that arises from it cannot be underestimated. As these countries vie for control over energy sources, tensions escalate, and the potential for conflict increases. The outcomes of these power struggles have far-reaching implications for global energy security and stability.

In conclusion, the antagonisms and jealousies of regional middle powers have a profound impact on global diplomacy and power dynamics. The competition for regional influence, economic rivalries, territorial disputes, political power struggles, cultural clashes, and energy competitions among these middle powers shape the contours of international relations. Understanding and effectively managing these dynamics is crucial for diplomats, economists, and strategists seeking to navigate the complex world of global politics and ensure peace, stability, and prosperity for all nations.

Sub-chapter heading

Sub-chapter heading: The Role of Regional Middle Powers in Regional Integration and Cooperation

In the ever-evolving landscape of global diplomacy and power dynamics, regional middle powers play a crucial role in shaping regional integration and cooperation. These countries, although not major global powers, possess significant influence and resources within their respective regions. Their actions and policies have far-reaching implications for the antagonisms and jealousies among regional players.

Regional middle powers, such as Brazil, South Africa, Turkey, and South Korea, have been actively engaged in regional integration initiatives. By leveraging their economic prowess, diplomatic acumen, and strategic location, these middle powers have become key drivers of regional cooperation. They recognize that regional integration is vital for achieving sustainable economic growth, enhancing political stability, and addressing shared challenges.

One notable example of regional integration spearheaded by middle powers is the establishment of trade blocs and economic partnerships. These initiatives aim to foster economic rivalries and trade disputes among regional middle powers, as well as strengthen their collective bargaining power on the global stage. By creating a common market and reducing trade barriers, middle powers can attract investments, stimulate trade, and boost economic development within their regions.

Moreover, middle powers often find themselves embroiled in territorial disputes and conflicts with their regional counterparts. These conflicts arise due to overlapping claims, historical grievances, or power struggles. However, these middle powers also recognize the importance of finding diplomatic solutions to these disputes. They understand that prolonged conflicts can hinder regional integration and cooperation, leading to a loss of economic opportunities and weakening their collective position in global affairs.

To counterbalance regional rivalries, middle powers form security alliances and devise counterbalancing strategies. By forging partnerships and alliances with like-minded regional players, they can deter aggression and maintain stability in their respective regions. These security alliances also serve as a means to counter the influence of major global powers in the region.

However, a significant challenge faced by regional middle powers is the clash of cultures and identities. The diverse cultural, religious, and linguistic backgrounds of these countries often create tensions and hinder cooperation. Middle powers must navigate these differences and find common ground to foster unity and cooperation among regional players.

Lastly, the competition for energy resources among regional middle powers adds another layer of complexity to their interactions. As global energy demand continues to rise, these middle powers vie for control over energy resources to bolster their economic growth and enhance their geopolitical standing. This competition can lead to conflicts and further exacerbate the antagonisms and jealousies among regional players.

In conclusion, regional middle powers play a critical role in regional integration and cooperation. Their actions and policies impact global diplomacy, power dynamics, and the overall security and stability of the international system. By understanding the implications of their conflicts, rivalries, and alliances, diplomats, economists, and strategists can gain valuable insights into the dynamics of regional middle powers and devise strategies to navigate and mitigate potential challenges.

Chapter 10: Role of Regional Middle Powers in Regional Integration and Cooperation

Efforts towards regional integration by middle powers

Regional integration has become a critical aspect of global diplomacy and power dynamics, with middle powers playing a significant role in shaping the outcomes. These middle powers, often situated between major global players, strive to bridge the gaps and foster cooperation among neighboring countries. This subchapter explores the efforts made by regional middle powers towards regional integration, highlighting the various challenges and opportunities they encounter.

One of the key aspects that middle powers address in their pursuit of regional integration is the antagonisms and jealousies among their peers. By engaging in diplomatic dialogues and mediating disputes, they aim to build trust and foster a sense of common purpose among regional actors. Through initiatives such as joint economic projects, cultural exchanges, and educational programs, middle powers create platforms that encourage cooperation and understanding.

The impact of regional middle powers on global diplomacy and power dynamics cannot be underestimated. Their ability to balance the interests of major powers and smaller states allows for more inclusive decision-making processes. By leveraging their diplomatic skills, middle powers can influence global negotiations and shape outcomes that benefit the region as a whole.

However, competition for regional influence among middle powers can hinder the progress of regional integration. Economic rivalries and trade disputes often emerge as a result of conflicting interests and differing economic strategies. These challenges require middle powers to find creative solutions and foster an environment of compromise and mutual benefit.

Territorial disputes and conflicts between regional middle powers can also impede regional integration efforts. However, by utilizing diplomatic channels, middle powers can mediate these disputes and facilitate dialogue towards peaceful resolutions. Political rivalries and power struggles can further complicate the situation, highlighting the need for strong leadership and cooperative frameworks.

Security alliances and counterbalancing strategies are crucial aspects of regional integration efforts. Middle powers often form alliances and partnerships to counter the influence of major powers and ensure regional stability. These alliances help create a sense of security and enable middle powers to address common challenges, such as terrorism and non-state actors.

Cultural and identity clashes among regional middle powers can pose significant challenges to regional integration. However, by promoting cultural exchanges, middle powers can foster a sense of shared identity and understanding. This can lead to increased cooperation and a more cohesive regional bloc.

The role of regional middle powers in regional integration and cooperation cannot be overstated. Through their diplomatic efforts and economic initiatives, middle powers can facilitate the integration of neighboring countries, leading to enhanced economic growth and political stability.

Energy resources and competition among regional middle powers are crucial factors in regional integration efforts. Middle powers often vie for control over energy resources, which can lead to tensions and conflicts. However, by adopting transparent and cooperative approaches, middle powers can harness these resources for the benefit of the entire region.

The implications of regional middle power conflicts on global security and stability are significant. As these conflicts can escalate and draw in major powers, the potential for wider regional and global instability increases. Therefore, the resolution of conflicts among regional middle powers is crucial for maintaining global security and stability.

In conclusion, middle powers play a vital role in regional integration efforts. Despite the challenges they face, their diplomatic skills, economic initiatives, and security alliances contribute to the creation of a more integrated and cooperative regional bloc. By addressing the antagonisms, economic rivalries, and territorial disputes among them, middle powers can pave the way for a more prosperous and stable future. This subchapter aims to provide valuable insights into the efforts made by middle powers towards regional integration and their impact on global diplomacy and power dynamics.

Regional cooperation initiatives led by middle powers

Regional cooperation initiatives led by middle powers play a crucial role in shaping global diplomacy, power dynamics, and regional integration. These initiatives are driven by the need for middle powers to assert their influence and counterbalance the dominance of major powers. In this subchapter, we will explore the various regional cooperation initiatives undertaken by middle powers and their implications on global security and stability.

One of the key aspects of regional cooperation initiatives led by middle powers is the competition for regional influence. Middle powers such as Brazil, India, and South Africa strive to enhance their regional role by forming alliances and partnerships with neighboring countries. These initiatives aim to promote economic growth, political stability, and cultural exchange. However, they can also lead to economic rivalries and trade disputes among regional middle powers, as they compete for access to markets and resources.

Territorial disputes and conflicts between regional middle powers are another significant factor that shapes regional cooperation initiatives. For instance, the ongoing territorial disputes in the South China Sea between China, Japan, and ASEAN countries have hindered regional integration efforts. These conflicts not only impact regional stability but also have implications for global security.

Political rivalries and power struggles among regional middle powers also influence regional cooperation initiatives. Countries like Iran, Saudi Arabia, and Turkey compete for influence in the Middle East, often leading to proxy conflicts and regional divisions. These power struggles can hinder efforts towards regional integration and cooperation.

On the other hand, security alliances and counterbalancing strategies among regional middle powers can contribute to regional stability. For example, the Quadrilateral Security Dialogue (Quad) between the United States, Japan, Australia, and India aims to maintain a free and open Indo-Pacific region. Such alliances can act as a counterbalance to the influence of major powers and ensure regional security.

Cultural and identity clashes among regional middle powers also impact regional cooperation initiatives. Differences in religion, language, and historical grievances can hinder collaboration and integration. Overcoming these cultural barriers is essential for fostering regional cooperation and stability.

Furthermore, the role of regional middle powers in regional integration and cooperation cannot be underestimated. Countries like Mexico, South Korea, and Indonesia actively participate in regional organizations such as ASEAN and the Pacific Alliance, promoting economic integration and political cooperation. These initiatives contribute to regional stability and enhance the influence of middle powers on the global stage.

Energy resources and competition among regional middle powers are also important factors influencing regional cooperation. Middle powers with abundant energy resources, such as Russia and Saudi Arabia, often use their energy reserves as a tool for regional influence. The competition for energy resources can lead to tensions and conflicts among regional middle powers.

In conclusion, regional cooperation initiatives led by middle powers have a significant impact on global diplomacy, power dynamics, and regional integration. While they can contribute to regional stability and economic growth, they are also influenced by antagonisms, rivalries, and conflicts among middle powers. Understanding these dynamics is crucial for diplomats, economists, and strategists to navigate the complexities of regional politics and foster global security and stability.

Sub-chapter heading

Sub-chapter Heading: Regional Middle Powers and Their Impact on Global Power Dynamics

In this sub-chapter, we delve into the intricate world of regional middle powers and explore the various antagonisms and jealousies that arise among these influential players. Addressing a diverse audience of diplomats, economists, and strategists, we aim to unravel the complex dynamics at play within this sphere, shedding light on the implications of their actions on global diplomacy and power balance.

Regional middle powers often find themselves engaged in a fierce competition for influence within their respective regions. We examine the factors driving this competition and the strategies employed by these powers to secure their positions. From economic rivalries and trade disputes to territorial conflicts and political power struggles, we analyze the multifaceted nature of their relationships.

One of the key aspects explored in this sub-chapter is the role of security alliances and counterbalancing strategies adopted by regional middle powers. We investigate how these alliances shape the regional power dynamics and influence global security and stability. Additionally, we delve into the cultural and identity clashes that often exacerbate these rivalries, further complicating the diplomatic landscape.

Furthermore, we shed light on the role of regional middle powers in regional integration and cooperation, examining their contributions to the development of regional organizations and the challenges they face in fostering unity among diverse nations. We also explore the impact of energy resources on the competition among these powers, as control over such resources often becomes a focal point of rivalry.

Finally, we conclude by examining the implications of conflicts among regional middle powers on global security and stability. We analyze how these conflicts can escalate and potentially disrupt the delicate balance of power on a global scale. By understanding the intricacies of these antagonisms and jealousies, diplomats, economists, and strategists can gain valuable insights into the dynamics that shape our world today.

In "Middle Power Maneuvers: Unraveling the Antagonisms and Jealousies of Regional Players," we offer a comprehensive analysis of the role played by regional middle powers, their impact on global diplomacy and power dynamics, and the various factors that drive their conflicts and rivalries.

Sub-chapter heading

Sub-chapter Heading: The Role of Regional Middle Powers in Regional Integration and Cooperation

In today's complex global landscape, regional middle powers play a crucial role in shaping regional integration and cooperation. These middle powers, often situated between major global players, possess unique characteristics and capabilities that enable them to exert influence and navigate the complexities of regional dynamics. This sub-chapter explores the significance of regional middle powers in promoting unity, stability, and development within their respective regions.

Regional middle powers are defined by their ability to project influence beyond their national borders, leveraging their economic, political, and diplomatic strengths. Their actions not only impact their immediate neighbors but also have far-reaching consequences for global diplomacy and power dynamics. As diplomats, economists, and strategists, it is crucial for us to understand the antagonisms and jealousies that arise among these regional powers and how they can be managed to foster cooperation and regional integration.

These middle powers often compete for regional influence, engaging in economic rivalries and trade disputes. By analyzing these rivalries, we can gain insights into their motivations and strategies, and identify potential avenues for collaboration and economic partnerships. Additionally, territorial disputes and conflicts between regional middle powers can disrupt stability and hinder regional integration efforts. Understanding the complexities of these disputes will enable us to identify diplomatic solutions and facilitate peaceful resolutions.

Political rivalries and power struggles among regional middle powers can also hinder regional integration and cooperation. By delving into the root causes of these rivalries, we can devise strategies to mitigate tensions and promote dialogue between conflicting parties. Furthermore, security alliances and counterbalancing strategies among regional middle powers shape the security landscape of their respective regions. It is crucial to analyze these alliances and understand their implications for global security and stability.

Cultural and identity clashes among regional middle powers can also impede regional integration efforts. By exploring the underlying cultural, religious, and historical factors that contribute to these clashes, we can identify common ground and promote understanding and cooperation.

Furthermore, the competition for energy resources among regional middle powers has significant implications for regional integration and global energy security. By examining these resource-driven competitions, we can identify potential areas for collaboration and resource sharing, fostering regional integration and stability.

In conclusion, the role of regional middle powers in regional integration and cooperation is vital in today's world. By understanding the antagonisms and jealousies that exist among these powers, we can devise strategies to promote collaboration, resolve conflicts, and foster stability. These efforts not only enhance regional integration but also have far-reaching implications for global diplomacy, power dynamics, security, and stability. As diplomats, economists, and strategists, it is crucial for us to explore these dynamics and collaborate with regional middle powers to shape a more peaceful, prosperous, and cooperative world.

Chapter 11: Energy Resources and Competition Among Regional Middle Powers

Importance of energy resources for regional middle powers

The Importance of Energy Resources for Regional Middle Powers

In today's globalized world, energy resources have become a vital component of a nation's power and influence. This is particularly true for regional middle powers, who often find themselves engaging in various conflicts, rivalries, and power struggles within their respective regions. Understanding the importance of energy resources in this context is crucial for diplomats, economists, and strategists seeking to unravel the antagonisms and jealousies of these regional players.

Energy resources play a significant role in determining the influence of regional middle powers on global diplomacy and power dynamics. As these nations possess valuable energy reserves, they can leverage their resources to gain diplomatic leverage and assert their interests on the international stage. The abundance of energy resources can enhance a nation's economic prowess and enable it to form alliances, negotiate favorable trade agreements, and exert influence over global energy markets.

Competition for regional influence among middle powers often revolves around access to energy resources. Scarce energy supplies can lead to economic rivalries and trade disputes among these nations. Additionally, territorial disputes and conflicts can arise as middle powers vie for control over energy-rich regions, further exacerbating political rivalries and power struggles. The ability to secure energy resources can be seen as a matter of national security, prompting middle powers to form security alliances and adopt counterbalancing strategies to protect their interests.

Furthermore, energy resources can also act as catalysts for cultural and identity clashes among regional middle powers. The exploitation and control of energy reserves can disrupt local communities, leading to social and cultural tensions. These clashes can further complicate regional integration and cooperation efforts, as countries prioritize their energy interests over collaborative endeavors.

The consequences of conflicts among regional middle powers extend beyond regional boundaries, impacting global security and stability. Energy resource disputes can lead to disruptions in the global energy supply chain, affecting economies worldwide. Moreover, tensions arising from energy rivalries can escalate into armed conflicts, posing threats to peace and stability on a global scale.

In conclusion, energy resources hold immense significance for regional middle powers. They shape the antagonisms and jealousies among these nations, influence global diplomacy and power dynamics, fuel competition for regional influence, and impact economic, territorial, political, and security dynamics. Recognizing the pivotal role of energy resources in the conflicts and rivalries of regional middle powers is vital for diplomats, economists, and strategists seeking to navigate and mitigate these complex dynamics, ultimately contributing to global security and stability.

Competition for energy resources and its implications

Energy resources play a crucial role in shaping the dynamics of global diplomacy and power struggles among regional middle powers. In this subchapter, we will explore the intense competition for energy resources and the various implications it has on regional and global stability.

The antagonisms or jealousies of regional middle powers are often fueled by their quest for energy resources. As these powers vie for control over vital energy reserves, tensions arise, leading to conflicts and rivalries that impact the geopolitical landscape. Understanding these antagonisms is crucial for diplomats, economists, and strategists in order to navigate the complex web of regional dynamics.

Regional middle powers exert a significant influence on global diplomacy and power dynamics. Their competition for regional influence often takes center stage, as they strategically align themselves with other nations to counterbalance opposing powers. This power struggle can escalate into economic rivalries and trade disputes, as middle powers seek to secure energy resources for their own economic growth and stability.

Territorial disputes and conflicts also arise among regional middle powers due to the competition for energy resources. Control over resource-rich areas becomes a catalyst for political rivalries and power struggles. Diplomats and strategists need to carefully analyze these conflicts and devise effective strategies to mitigate tensions and maintain regional stability.

Security alliances and counterbalancing strategies are frequently employed by middle powers to protect their energy interests. These alliances not only shape regional dynamics but also have implications for global security and stability. Understanding the intricacies of these alliances is crucial for diplomats and strategists seeking to maintain a balance of power in regions marked by energy resource competition.

Furthermore, cultural and identity clashes often underpin the competition among regional middle powers. Differences in values, traditions, and societal norms can exacerbate tensions, making it imperative for diplomats and strategists to navigate these clashes to ensure peaceful cooperation and regional integration.

The role of regional middle powers in regional integration and cooperation cannot be underestimated. Their active participation in energy-related projects and initiatives can foster economic growth, enhance diplomatic relations, and promote stability. Understanding the dynamics of regional integration is key for diplomats and strategists seeking to harness the potential of middle powers for sustainable development.

Lastly, the implications of conflicts among regional middle powers on global security and stability cannot be overlooked. The competition for energy resources can destabilize entire regions, leading to political unrest, economic volatility, and even armed conflicts. Finding effective ways to address these implications is vital for diplomats, economists, and strategists to ensure a secure and stable global order.

In conclusion, the competition for energy resources among regional middle powers has far-reaching implications for regional and global diplomacy, power dynamics, and security. Understanding these implications is crucial for diplomats, economists, and strategists in order to navigate the complexities of regional conflicts, foster peaceful cooperation, and maintain global stability.

Sub-chapter heading

Sub-chapter Heading: The Impact of Regional Middle Powers on Global Diplomacy and Power Dynamics

In today's complex global landscape, regional middle powers have emerged as pivotal players, wielding significant influence and shaping the course of international affairs. This sub-chapter delves into the multifaceted impact of these regional actors on global diplomacy and power dynamics, unraveling the intricacies of their interactions with major powers and their role in shaping the future of international relations.

The antagonisms or jealousies of regional middle powers lay bare the inherent tensions that arise when these actors vie for influence and assert their own interests. With their growing economic prowess and strategic significance, these regional players find themselves in competition with one another, often leading to economic rivalries and trade disputes. This chapter examines the consequences of such conflicts, exploring how they not only impact regional stability but also reverberate across the global trade landscape.

Territorial disputes and conflicts between regional middle powers further complicate the geopolitical landscape, posing challenges to both regional and global stability. Through in-depth analysis, this sub-chapter explores the underlying causes of these conflicts and their implications for global security and stability. It also sheds light on the role of political rivalries and power struggles among regional middle powers, dissecting the dynamics that shape alliances and counterbalancing strategies.

Cultural and identity clashes among regional middle powers add yet another layer of complexity to the global diplomatic arena. This sub-chapter examines how cultural differences and identity politics shape regional dynamics and explores the potential for cooperation or conflict stemming from these disparities. Moreover, it highlights the role of regional middle powers in regional integration and cooperation, showcasing the potential for collaboration amidst these diversities.

Energy resources and competition among regional middle powers have become critical issues in global politics. This sub-chapter delves into the strategic importance of energy resources and analyzes how their competition among regional middle powers impacts global energy security.

By delving into these various aspects, this sub-chapter aims to provide diplomats, economists, and strategists with a comprehensive understanding of the impact of regional middle powers on global diplomacy and power dynamics. It elucidates the intricate web of rivalries, alliances, and conflicts among these actors, equipping the readers with the knowledge required to navigate the evolving landscape of international relations. Ultimately, it underscores the significance of regional middle powers in shaping the trajectory of global politics and calls for a nuanced approach to understanding and engaging with these influential players.

Sub-chapter heading

Sub-chapter Heading: The Impact of Regional Middle Powers on Global Diplomacy and Power Dynamics

In the complex realm of international relations, regional middle powers have emerged as influential actors, capable of shaping global diplomacy and power dynamics. This sub-chapter delves into the crucial role these middle powers play in the international arena, addressing the various aspects and implications of their actions.

One of the key focuses of this sub-chapter is exploring the antagonisms and jealousies that often arise among regional middle powers. As these states vie for regional influence, their competition can lead to tensions and rivalries. We examine the underlying causes and manifestations of these antagonisms, shedding light on the intricate dynamics at play.

Furthermore, we analyze the economic rivalries and trade disputes that frequently arise among regional middle powers. As these states compete for economic dominance, conflicts can arise, impacting not only their own economies but also the global trade landscape. We delve into the implications of these rivalries and the strategies employed by these powers to gain a competitive edge.

Territorial disputes and conflicts between regional middle powers receive particular attention in this sub-chapter. These disputes often stem from historical, political, and cultural factors, and can have far-reaching consequences. We examine how these conflicts impact regional stability and explore potential avenues for resolution.

Political rivalries and power struggles among regional middle powers are also explored, as these states seek to assert their influence and shape the political landscape within their regions. We analyze the strategies employed by these powers to gain political advantage and the implications of these rivalries on regional integration and cooperation.

Security alliances and counterbalancing strategies adopted by regional middle powers are another crucial aspect addressed in this sub-chapter. We examine how these alliances shape power dynamics and influence global security and stability.

Additionally, we delve into the cultural and identity clashes that often occur among regional middle powers. These clashes can exacerbate existing tensions and further complicate diplomatic relations. We explore the impact of cultural differences and identity politics on regional cooperation and integration.

Lastly, this sub-chapter investigates the role of regional middle powers in regional integration and cooperation. We analyze how these powers can act as catalysts for cooperation and examine the implications of their involvement in regional integration efforts.

In summary, this sub-chapter provides an in-depth analysis of the impact of regional middle powers on global diplomacy and power dynamics. By exploring the various dimensions of their actions, from economic rivalries to security alliances, cultural clashes to territorial disputes, this sub-chapter offers valuable insights into the intricate web of relations that define the international system. Diplomats, economists, and strategists will find this analysis essential in understanding the implications of regional middle power conflicts on global security and stability.

Chapter 12: Implications of Regional Middle Power Conflicts on Global Security and Stability

Global ramifications of conflicts among regional middle powers

Conflicts among regional middle powers have far-reaching consequences that extend beyond their immediate regions. These power struggles and rivalries between nations have significant global ramifications, impacting various aspects of diplomacy, power dynamics, economies, and security. In this subchapter, we will delve into the complex web of antagonisms and jealousies among regional middle powers, their impact on global affairs, and the implications for diplomats, economists, and strategists.

One of the key areas affected by conflicts among regional middle powers is global diplomacy and power dynamics. These conflicts often result in shifting alliances, as middle powers seek to counterbalance the influence of their rivals. Diplomats must navigate these intricate relationships and understand the implications for their own countries' foreign policies. Economists, on the other hand, must assess the potential economic repercussions of these conflicts, such as trade disputes and economic rivalries, which can disrupt global markets and supply chains.

Competition for regional influence is another significant consequence of conflicts among middle powers. As regional players vie for dominance, they engage in a race to secure strategic alliances, gain access to resources, and expand their spheres of influence. This competition can escalate tensions and lead to territorial disputes and conflicts, with serious implications for global security and stability. Strategists must analyze these power struggles and devise counterbalancing strategies to prevent further escalation and maintain equilibrium in the international system.

Cultural and identity clashes are often at the root of conflicts among regional middle powers. These clashes can exacerbate existing rivalries and make resolution more challenging. Understanding the cultural dynamics at play is crucial for diplomats and strategists seeking to mediate or mitigate these conflicts. Additionally, the role of regional middle powers in regional integration and cooperation becomes vital in fostering dialogue and promoting peaceful resolutions.

Furthermore, economic rivalries and energy resource competition among regional middle powers have a direct impact on global energy markets and resource allocation. Diplomats and economists must monitor these dynamics closely, as disruptions in energy supplies or disputes over resources can have significant implications for global energy security and economic stability.

In conclusion, conflicts among regional middle powers have extensive global ramifications. From their impact on global diplomacy and power dynamics to economic rivalries, territorial disputes, and security alliances, these conflicts shape the international landscape. Understanding these dynamics is essential for diplomats, economists, and strategists who seek to navigate the complexities of global affairs and maintain peace, stability, and prosperity in an ever-changing world.

Potential risks and challenges for global security

In the ever-evolving landscape of international relations, the role of regional middle powers has become increasingly significant. These countries, with their growing economies and expanding influence, often find themselves entangled in a web of antagonisms and jealousies with their neighboring counterparts. This subchapter aims to shed light on the potential risks and challenges that these dynamics pose for global security.

One of the key risks lies in the impact of regional middle powers on global diplomacy and power dynamics. As these countries strive to assert their influence on the world stage, they may inadvertently disrupt the delicate balance of power, leading to increased tensions and the potential for conflict. Diplomats and strategists must carefully navigate these power struggles to maintain stability and avoid escalation.

Competition for regional influence among middle powers also poses a risk to global security. Economic rivalries and trade disputes can quickly spiral out of control, leading to a breakdown in diplomatic relations and even economic warfare. The interconnectedness of the global economy means that any disruptions in regional trade have far-reaching consequences, impacting not only the involved parties but also the global economic stability.

Territorial disputes and conflicts between regional middle powers further exacerbate the risks to global security. These conflicts can quickly escalate, drawing in other nations and potentially sparking wider regional conflicts. Diplomats and strategists must work tirelessly to find peaceful resolutions to these disputes and prevent them from spiraling into full-blown conflicts.

Political rivalries and power struggles among regional middle powers also have implications for global security. These rivalries may result in proxy wars or the formation of security alliances and counterbalancing strategies, which can further destabilize regions and strain diplomatic relations. The potential for miscalculations and misunderstandings between these powers adds an additional layer of complexity to the security landscape.

Cultural and identity clashes among regional middle powers also pose challenges to global security. These disputes often stem from historical grievances and can fuel nationalism and separatist movements, leading to internal conflicts and regional instability. Diplomats and strategists must understand the underlying causes of these clashes and work towards promoting dialogue and understanding to mitigate the risks they pose.

The role of regional middle powers in regional integration and cooperation is another aspect that impacts global security. Their ability to bridge gaps and facilitate dialogue between nations is crucial for maintaining stability. However, if these middle powers fail to effectively manage regional integration and cooperation, it can lead to increased tensions and security risks.

Lastly, the competition for energy resources among regional middle powers presents a significant challenge for global security. As these countries vie for control over vital resources, conflicts may arise, leading to disruptions in the global energy supply chain and potential economic crises.

In conclusion, the risks and challenges for global security posed by regional middle powers are multi-faceted and complex. Diplomats, economists, and strategists must carefully analyze and navigate these dynamics to ensure stability and peace in an increasingly interconnected world. Failure to do so could have far-reaching consequences for global security and stability.

Sub-chapter heading

Sub-chapter Heading: The Impact of Regional Middle Powers on Global Diplomacy and Power Dynamics

In today's complex and interconnected world, regional middle powers have emerged as key players in shaping global diplomacy and power dynamics. This sub-chapter delves into the various ways in which the antagonisms and jealousies among these middle powers have far-reaching consequences for the international community.

The antagonisms or jealousies of regional middle powers have the potential to disrupt global diplomacy and power dynamics. As these powers seek to assert their regional influence, competition becomes inevitable. This sub-chapter explores the nature of these rivalries and their implications for the balance of power on a global scale.

Economic rivalries and trade disputes among regional middle powers further complicate the diplomatic landscape. With economic interdependence at an all-time high, conflicts arising from trade imbalances, protectionism, or market access can have ripple effects across the globe. This sub-chapter examines the economic dimensions of middle power maneuvers and the consequences for international trade and investment.

Territorial disputes and conflicts between regional middle powers are another source of contention with significant global implications. The sub-chapter explores the underlying causes of these conflicts, their potential to destabilize entire regions, and the strategies employed by middle powers to assert their territorial claims.

Political rivalries and power struggles among regional middle powers also shape global diplomacy. This sub-chapter analyzes the intricate dynamics of political competition between these powers, including their efforts to build alliances, counterbalance each other's influence, and project their own political ideologies.

Security alliances and counterbalancing strategies of regional middle powers are crucial components of the global security architecture. This sub-chapter examines the security implications of middle power maneuvers and the strategies employed to maintain regional stability and deter potential adversaries.

Cultural and identity clashes among regional middle powers can further exacerbate tensions and rivalries. This sub-chapter explores the role of cultural differences, historical grievances, and identity politics in shaping the behavior of middle powers, and the implications for regional integration and cooperation.

Furthermore, the sub-chapter delves into the role of regional middle powers in regional integration and cooperation. As these powers seek to maximize their influence, they often engage in efforts to foster regional alliances and enhance cooperation. The sub-chapter examines the motivations behind these actions and the potential for regional integration to shape global power dynamics.

Lastly, the sub-chapter analyzes the role of energy resources and competition among regional middle powers. With the growing demand for energy and the increasing importance of energy security, conflicts over resources can have significant implications for global stability. This sub-chapter explores the strategies employed by middle powers to secure energy resources and the consequences for global energy dynamics.

By shedding light on these various dimensions, this sub-chapter aims to provide diplomats, economists, and strategists with a comprehensive understanding of the impact of regional middle powers on global diplomacy and power dynamics. It underscores the need for a nuanced approach to managing the antagonisms and jealousies among these powers to ensure global security and stability.

Sub-chapter heading

Sub-chapter Heading: The Impact of Regional Middle Powers on Global Diplomacy and Power Dynamics

In the ever-evolving landscape of international relations, regional middle powers have emerged as significant players, exerting their influence and shaping global diplomacy and power dynamics. This sub-chapter explores the multifaceted impacts these middle powers have on the global stage, highlighting the complexities of their interactions and the consequences for global security and stability.

At the heart of their actions lie the antagonisms and jealousies among regional middle powers, driven by their desire to secure their own interests while competing for regional influence. These rivalries, rooted in economic, political, and territorial disputes, have the potential to disrupt global diplomacy and power structures, requiring careful navigation and strategic maneuvering.

Economic rivalries and trade disputes among regional middle powers further complicate the picture. As these powers vie for economic dominance, tensions rise, and trade barriers are erected. This not only hampers regional integration and cooperation but also has broader implications for global trade and economic stability.

Territorial disputes and conflicts between regional middle powers pose another significant challenge. Competing claims over land, maritime boundaries, and resources fuel tensions, escalating into potential flashpoints that threaten regional and global security. Diplomatic finesse and conflict resolution mechanisms are crucial to prevent these conflicts from spiraling out of control.

Political rivalries and power struggles among regional middle powers add another layer of complexity. As these powers vie for leadership and influence, proxy wars and covert operations become tools of choice, affecting not only regional stability but also global security. Understanding the underlying motivations and employing effective diplomatic strategies is essential to mitigate the risks posed by these rivalries.

Security alliances and counterbalancing strategies adopted by regional middle powers are vital in shaping power dynamics and maintaining regional stability. By forging alliances and partnerships, these powers seek to counterbalance the influence of major global players, ensuring their own security and protecting their interests.

Cultural and identity clashes among regional middle powers further complicate regional integration and cooperation efforts. As diverse cultural and religious identities intersect, tensions arise, hindering progress towards shared goals. Navigating these clashes requires a nuanced understanding of the complexities at play, and the promotion of dialogue and mutual understanding.

Finally, the role of regional middle powers in regional integration and cooperation cannot be understated. By leveraging their economic, political, and diplomatic influence, these powers play a pivotal role in fostering cooperation, resolving conflicts, and advancing regional integration initiatives. Their active engagement can lead to increased stability and prosperity for the region and beyond.

In conclusion, the impact of regional middle powers on global diplomacy and power dynamics is multifaceted and far-reaching. Their antagonisms, rivalries, and alliances shape the course of international relations, influencing global security, trade, and stability. Understanding these dynamics is essential for diplomats, economists, and strategists as they navigate the complexities of a world where regional middle powers are increasingly influential.

Chapter 13: Conclusion

Summary of key findings

In "Middle Power Maneuvers: Unraveling the Antagonisms and Jealousies of Regional Players," we delve into the intricate world of regional middle powers and their impact on global diplomacy, power dynamics, and regional integration. This subchapter, "Summary of Key Findings," presents a comprehensive overview of our research findings, providing valuable insights for diplomats, economists, and strategists alike.

1. The Antagonisms or Jealousies of Regional Middle Powers:

Our study reveals that regional middle powers frequently experience antagonisms and jealousies due to competing interests, historical rivalries, and aspirations for regional dominance. These dynamics often hinder cooperation and impede regional integration efforts.

2. The Impact of Regional Middle Powers on Global Diplomacy and Power Dynamics:

We find that regional middle powers play a crucial role in shaping global diplomacy and power dynamics. Their strategic alliances, counterbalancing strategies, and diplomatic maneuvering have a significant impact on international relations, influencing both regional and global outcomes.

3. Competition for Regional Influence among Middle Powers:

Our research highlights the intense competition for regional influence among middle powers. Economic rivalries, trade disputes, and cultural clashes often exacerbate tensions, leading to a constant struggle for dominance within the region.

4. Territorial Disputes and Conflicts between Regional Middle Powers:

Territorial disputes and conflicts are common among regional middle powers. These disputes not only pose threats to regional stability but also have wider implications for global security, as they often draw in major powers seeking to exploit these conflicts for their own strategic interests.

5. Political Rivalries and Power Struggles among Regional Middle Powers:

The quest for political supremacy among regional middle powers fuels power struggles and rivalries. These internal dynamics, combined with external pressures, often result in fragile political landscapes and hinder regional cooperation efforts.

6. Security Alliances and Counterbalancing Strategies of Regional Middle Powers:

Our research identifies the formation of security alliances and counterbalancing strategies as key responses by regional middle powers to mitigate external threats. These alliances help maintain a balance of power and safeguard their respective interests.

7. Cultural and Identity Clashes among Regional Middle Powers:

Cultural and identity clashes among regional middle powers can hinder effective cooperation and integration. These clashes often fuel nationalism and exacerbate existing tensions, making regional collaboration a complex endeavor.

8. Role of Regional Middle Powers in Regional Integration and Cooperation:

Despite the challenges they face, regional middle powers play a pivotal role in regional integration and cooperation. Their diplomatic efforts, economic influence, and soft power capabilities contribute to shaping regional frameworks and fostering cooperation among neighboring countries.

9. Energy Resources and Competition among Regional Middle Powers:

Our study highlights the fierce competition among regional middle powers for energy resources. The control and access to these resources not only impact their economic standing but also influence regional stability and global energy dynamics.

10. Implications of Regional Middle Power Conflicts on Global Security and Stability:

Finally, our research underscores the significant implications of conflicts among regional middle powers on global security and stability. The ripple effects of these conflicts can disrupt international relations, trigger power shifts, and potentially escalate into wider regional or global confrontations.

In conclusion, "Middle Power Maneuvers" sheds light on the intricate dynamics of regional middle powers and their impact on global diplomacy, power dynamics, and regional integration. This subchapter's key findings provide valuable insights for diplomats, economists, and strategists, enabling them to navigate the complexities of regional rivalries and drive effective policies that promote stability and cooperation.

Implications and recommendations for diplomats, economists, and strategists

In this subchapter, titled "Implications and Recommendations for Diplomats, Economists, and Strategists," we delve into the multifaceted implications of regional middle power dynamics and offer valuable recommendations for professionals in the fields of diplomacy, economics, and strategy. The chapter addresses the various niches associated with the antagonisms and jealousies of regional middle powers, their impact on global diplomacy and power dynamics, competition for regional influence, economic rivalries and trade disputes, territorial conflicts, political rivalries and power struggles, security alliances and counterbalancing strategies, cultural and identity clashes, role in regional integration and cooperation, energy resources, and implications on global security and stability.

For diplomats, understanding the intricacies of regional middle power dynamics is crucial. They must develop a nuanced understanding of the underlying antagonisms and jealousies that drive these regional players. This knowledge can help diplomats navigate complex diplomatic negotiations, mediate disputes, and foster dialogue between conflicting parties. Additionally, diplomats should actively promote regional integration and cooperation, encouraging middle powers to find common ground and work towards shared goals.

Economists must pay attention to the economic rivalries and trade disputes among regional middle powers. By identifying the areas of competition and potential collaboration, economists can provide valuable insights on the economic implications of these rivalries. They should explore opportunities for trade diversification and investment cooperation, helping middle powers leverage their economic strengths for mutual growth and prosperity.

Strategists need to analyze the territorial disputes and conflicts between regional middle powers. By understanding the underlying drivers and historical contexts of these conflicts, strategists can develop effective strategies to prevent escalation and promote peaceful resolutions. They should also assess the security alliances and counterbalancing strategies employed by these middle powers, identifying potential areas of collaboration and the implications for regional and global security.

Furthermore, all professionals in these fields should recognize the significance of cultural and identity clashes among regional middle powers. By promoting cultural understanding and fostering dialogue, they can contribute to building bridges and mitigating conflicts that arise from cultural differences. Finally, the implications of regional middle power conflicts on global security and stability cannot be ignored. Professionals in these fields should actively engage in efforts to prevent conflicts from spilling over and destabilizing global order, ensuring that international institutions and frameworks are robust enough to handle the challenges posed by these middle powers.

In conclusion, this subchapter offers valuable insights and recommendations for diplomats, economists, and strategists. By understanding the implications of regional middle power dynamics and working towards cooperation and conflict resolution, professionals in these fields can contribute to a more stable and prosperous global order.

Future research directions

Future research directions in the study of middle power maneuvers are essential to further understanding the complexities and dynamics of regional players. This subchapter explores potential areas for future investigation, providing a roadmap for diplomats, economists, and strategists interested in this field.

1. The antagonisms or jealousies of regional middle powers: Future research should delve into the root causes and underlying factors that

contribute to antagonisms and jealousies among middle powers in specific regions. Understanding the historical, cultural, and geopolitical contexts will shed light on the dynamics of these rivalries.

2. The impact of regional middle powers on global diplomacy and power dynamics: Research should focus on how the actions of regional middle powers influence global diplomacy and power dynamics. Exploring their role in shaping international agendas, forming alliances, and exerting influence on global issues will provide valuable insights.

3. Competition for regional influence among middle powers: Investigating the strategies employed by middle powers to gain regional influence and analyzing the consequences of such competition will enrich our understanding of regional dynamics.

4. Economic rivalries and trade disputes among regional middle powers: Future research should examine the economic rivalries and trade disputes between middle powers and their implications for regional stability and economic integration.

5. Territorial disputes and conflicts between regional middle powers: Understanding the causes, escalation, and resolution of territorial disputes and conflicts among middle powers will contribute to conflict prevention and resolution strategies.

6. Political rivalries and power struggles among regional middle powers: Analyzing the political rivalries and power struggles among middle powers will help identify the underlying factors and potential solutions to mitigate tensions.

7. Security alliances and counterbalancing strategies of regional middle powers: Research should explore the formation and impact of security alliances and counterbalancing strategies among middle powers and their effects on regional stability and global security.

8. Cultural and identity clashes among regional middle powers: Investigating the cultural and identity clashes that may exist among middle powers will provide insights into potential sources of tension and ways to foster cooperation.

9. Role of regional middle powers in regional integration and cooperation: Future research should explore the role of middle powers in regional integration and cooperation initiatives, analyzing their contributions and challenges faced in fostering regional unity.

10. Energy resources and competition among regional middle powers: Investigating the competition for energy resources among middle powers will provide an understanding of the implications for regional stability and global energy security.

11. Implications of regional middle power conflicts on global security and stability: Research should explore the potential consequences of conflicts between regional middle powers on global security and stability, examining the role of external actors in mitigating or exacerbating these conflicts.

By addressing these future research directions, scholars and practitioners can deepen their understanding of middle power maneuvers, contributing to more informed decision-making and the development of effective strategies in regional and global diplomacy.